D1519098

Langston
HUGHES
and
Gwendolyn
BROOKS

a reference guide

A
Reference
Publication
in
Literature

Ronald Gottesman
Editor

Langston
HUGHES
and
Gwendolyn
BROOKS

a reference guide

R. BAXTER MILLER

George Prior Publishers, London, England

G.K.HALL &CO.
70 LINCOLN STREET, BOSTON, MASS.

Available for sale in the British Commonwealth from
George Prior Publishers, 2 Rugby St., London, England
ISBN (U.K.)   0-86043-240-8

Library of Congress Cataloging in Publication Data
Miller, R. Baxter.
   Langston Hughes and Gwendolyn Brooks.

   (A reference publication in literature)
   Includes index.
   1. Hughes, Langston, 1902-1967 — Bibliography.
2. Brooks, Gwendolyn, 1917 — Bibliography.   I. Title.
II. Series: Reference publications in literature.
Z8423.3.M54   [PS3515.U274]   016.811'5'2   78-8272
ISBN 0-8161-7810-0

This publication is printed on permanent/durable acid-free paper
MANUFACTURED IN THE UNITED STATES OF AMERICA

Dedications

For Langston Hughes and Gwendolyn Brooks
  who have had different modes and, to an extent, different times.
  They have shown, nevertheless, the same humanity.

For some rare scholars and teachers, first at North Carolina Central
University and then at Brown
  By their enthusiasm, they taught me that research can complement
  imagination.

For the late Randolph Worsley, of Rocky Mount, N.C., my teacher
in the seventh grade
  In 1960 he brought a poem by Langston Hughes to his class.
  Of his generation, he was rare in integrating Black materials into his
  curriculum. A student late for class wanted to know if Mr. Worsley
  was going to send him to the principal's office. The wise man replied:
    Come here boy! I saw you when your bicycle rolled up on the
    schoolyard and know how much you love it; saw you running
    around the corner of the building; heard you climbing the stairs;
    imagined you breathing with all the breath within you; heard you
    coming down the hall in a last effort to attain. No boy! I am not
    going to send you to the office today because I want you to
    always try! Try hard!

  I thank these people for their gift of vision.

Contents

Introduction

Blackness Universal?: Perspective on the Critics of Langston Hughes and Gwendolyn Brooks

I. DIFFERENTILITY AND CONTINUITY

At first glance it would seem easier to contrast Langston Hughes
with Gwendolyn Brooks than to compare them. They matured in different
decades, and their writing has shown different styles. When the race-
consciousness and lyricism of Weary Blues (1926) helped to bring in
the Harlem (Negro) Renaissance, Hughes (1902-1967) was twenty-four.
Brooks (1917-   ) on the other hand, became twenty-four during the
early years of World War II, long after the Renaissance--if not its
influence--had ended. By lyrics such as "The Negro Speaks of Rivers"
(1921) and "Note on Commercial Theater" (1940), Hughes tried to communicate his epic sense. His forte was not a dramatic interaction of
characters but a portrait of the collective "I," which, for him, sym-
bolized the Black race that had endured. His literary examples came
from the tradition of liberated form such as Whitman, Sandburg,
Masters, and Lindsay; hers, at first, were the modern imagists such
as Pound and Eliot, although her verse later became more Whitmanesque.

Yet in a deeper sense, Hughes and Brooks shared common virtues.
Both were black midwesterners by birth--Hughes in Joplin, Missouri;
Brooks in Topeka, Kansas--and each achieved national recognition.
Both spoke so truly about the paradox of Black religion, and the irony
of American life that they made these themes universal. Their motifs
emerged not from self-denial but through self-fulfillment. For
Hughes and Brooks, art did more than resist social injustice: it
reaffirmed a higher moral principle. Both writers withstood social
pressures that tested their creative imaginations. Hughes lived
through the depression of the thirties and the backlash of the sixties, and during the early forties as well as fifties, Brooks withstood some critics' encouragement to write esoterically.

Introduction

Finally, both writers remained true to themselves. In "Daybreak in Alabama," the last poem of The Panther and the Lash, Hughes's persona renewed an optimistic vision, just as Brooks's did in "Second Sermon on the warpland," the last verse in Mecca. While Richard Wright, Chester Himes, and James Baldwin were in France, Hughes and Brooks continued to write in America. They avoided Ralph Ellison's strange silence--which may signal loss of heart more than loss of imagination--a sad foreshadowing perhaps of Imamu Baraka (formerly LeRoi Jones). For more than forty years Hughes displayed conviction and integrity, and for more than thirty-two Brooks has shown hers. The purpose here is not to trace the vision of either writer but to examine the scholars and critics who have written about both.

Because Hughes was active during the Harlem Renaissance, his work received critical acclaim two decades before Brooks published Street in Bronzeville (hereafter Street). His work continued to earn attention in the forties and fifties when Brooks found herself a woman without an audience. The criticism of the sixties, which stressed the racial importance of Hughes, also gave Brooks's poetry its first major analyses. Writers of the seventies look on Hughes in retrospect, acknowledging him as one whose literature will endure, and they are now beginning to speak about Brooks's work in the same way. Scholarship about these two authors reflects diverse critical approaches. By reading the relevant secondary materials, one realizes that critical pluralism--an evaluation that combines formal analysis, history, sociology, archetype, and morality--will clarify these writers' rhetorical power and their meanings.

II. LANGSTON HUGHES

The scholarship of the twenties emphasized comparison to contemporaries, innovative usage of music, and evaluation of Black dialect. Examples of this first kind came from Robert T. Klein (1924.B2) and by Countee Cullen (1926.B2) who was ambivalent toward his fellow poet. Two observers, W. E. B. DuBois (1924.B1) and Du Bose Heyward (1926.B4; 1927.B4), praised Hughes's originality in using jazz and blues forms. Showing a need for stereotype, Herbert Gorman said that one could not compare Hughes with Humbert Wolfe or Richard Addington, since Hughes was "colored." Gorman then cited the Blues poems that gave (to him) a "vivid sensation of the Negro spirit." Alain Locke, on the other hand, made comments about Hughes's folk style that were less demeaning. For him Hughes represented much: "not the ragged provincialism of a minstrel but the descriptive detachment of a Vachel Lindsay and Sandburg...the democratic sweep and universality of a Whitman."

Praise of dialect, like praise of Blues, was double-edged. Consider Elizabeth Sergeant's remarks that Hughes's style was colloquial, casual, and fervent--in the "manner of the race" (1926.B6). Babette

Deutsch (1927.B2), by contrast, complimented Hughes's high craftsmanship and his conscious usage of illiteracy which transcended old stereotypes. Kenneth Fearing (1927.B3) argued that Hughes was unfamiliar with the American language, and Julia Peterkin (1927.B8) also admired Hughes's colloquial manner. Without the use of conventional forms, she said, he created universal comedy, tragedy, and despair. One might expect these different opinions about Hughes's uses of dialect, since folk diction provoked much controversy in literary circles. Often Black critics condemned Fine Clothes to the Jew (1927) because they believed that it illustrated the imperfections of their race. But Hughes portrayed neither stereotype nor Black mask (as Dunbar occasionally did). Rather, in looking beneath both, he located some genuinely human qualities.

If the scholarship of the 1920's placed Hughes in the context of the Harlem Renaissance, that of the 1930's looked back on that period. One might have expected James Weldon Johnson to agree with Cullen, since Johnson (1930.B5), also recognized that Hughes was a rebel in content and form. Yet Johnson's tone was harsher than Cullen's. Hughes, according to Johnson, took subjects from the gutter. Johnson quickly and ambivalently added that Hughes's effects, while different from Cullen's, had "equal finality." J. Saunders Redding (1930.B6) also saw Hughes as contrasting with Cullen, those two creative writers representing then the extremes of Black American poetry. Toward the end of the decade (1938.B1), Norman McLeod described Hughes as a man who maintained honesty and sincerity during the Renaissance as well as a folk poet who felt more than thought. For McLeod, Hughes's empathy with Blacks rang more true than his empathy with the working class.

The Great Depression occurred during the thirties, and much of the scholarship of that decade was Marxist. Lydia Filatova (1933.B1) thought that Hughes was the only established Black writer whose work deviated from the bourgeois. In breaking with the Harlem tradition, according to her, he became a realist. He was the "first revolutionary poet of the Negro proletariate." In her word "realistic," one could discern a major danger of Marxist critics on Hughes. They demanded social prerequisites of art, and they began critical analysis by seeking these prerequisites. Would one have done better to ask what the work implicitly intended? Because the Marxists appreciated only one kind of literature, the documentary, they often ignored the creative and mythmaking faculties. In the thirties this limitation was as conspicuous as in the seventies when the most extreme followers of the "Black Aesthetic" would link literature to politics, as opposed to linking politics to literature.

Often the articles or reviews of the thirties focused on Not Without Laughter (1930) and Ways of White Folks (1934 [hereafter White Folks]). As for the first, an anonymous reviewer (1930.B1) appreciated its realism as well as its treatment of character, and Herschel Brickell (1930.B2) discovered a tender understanding.

V. F. Calverton, possibly the most often quoted reviewer of Hughes's work, noted both the weaknesses and strengths of the novel. While observing that the structure of the book should be tighter, he praised Hughes's characterization and charm. For him the book lacked any rigor of style or sustained intensity, but maintained a quiet beauty. In Walt Carmon's review (1930.B4), the reader could sense the Marxist critics who favored integrationism and feared Black Nationalism. First Carmon noted the cliches. Not Without Laughter, he said, contributed to Black American and proletarian literature, and it digressed from the tradition of "Negro Burlesque" sponsored by Carl Van Vechten. Did Carmon discover something Marxism could not explain? Race clouded class, he said; bitterness and hatred were misdirected at the white race as a whole. Despite his contentions, however, the novel did show social class. The problem was that Not Without Laughter forced Carmon to experience such class through the eyes of Sandy Williams, a Black American. Because Carmon could not, the trouble that he found reflected his own. Mary Ross (1930.B7) liked the verisimilitude of the book and its fidelity to life; Sterling Brown (1937.B1) called it one of the best novels by a black author and a good novel about boyhood.

As with Not Without Laughter critics commended White Folks. For Sherwood Anderson Hughes's Negroes were "alive and warm," but Hughes's whites "pretentious and fake": "Mr. Hughes, my hat is off to you in relation to your own race, but not mine" (1934.B1). Of the many reviewers or essayists over a half-century of criticism, Anderson probably sensed Hughes's achievement most deeply. Hughes's effort was to create an American romance that reversed the traditional roles of Whites and Blacks. Hughes created counter-culture and counter-mythology, and Sherwood Anderson laughed at the recognition.

Others reviewed White Folks favorably. Herschell Brickell (1931.B1) noted that it contained some of the best stories to appear in the country. To him the book strengthened Hughes's reputation as the most talented Black American writer. Saying that Hughes had fulfilled his [Hughes's] early promise, Horace Gregory (1934.B3) agreed. Despite its race and class consciousness, said Gregory, White Folks transcended documentary literature, and Hughes undermined the traditional dichotomy between propaganda and art. While sharing Sherwood Anderson's observation, Martha Greuning's criticism lacked his humor. Although to her the whites in the book appeared sordid, cruel, silly, and unsentimental, the best stories excelled. Alain Locke believed that the stories challenged all who wanted to define the race question (1934.B6), and that their most illuminating moods came from caustic satire. In finding White Folks to be Hughes's strongest work (1934.B7), Vernon Loggins indirectly supported Locke's compliments. Finally George Streator (1934.B8) contradicted the Marxist critics: Did Hughes not laugh at whites of all social classes? No story in White Folks, said Streator, was as revolutionary as Hughes was portrayed as being, and the struggles illustrated there occured because of race. Possibly Streator carried his point too far, since

"Father to Son," one story, had revolutionary implications. But he
presented the Marxists with a formidable argument. For a Black American writer, race was class and had priority.

For Hughes in the 1940's the scholarly emphasis was still on tradition. Ruth Lechlinter (1947.B3) continued to contrast his colloquialism with Cullen's formality. Bertram L. Woodruff (1947.B4),
on the contrary, found that Hughes and Cullen shared the same religion.
In Negro Voices in American Fiction (1948.B2), a definitive work,
Hugh M. Gloster remembered Hughes's alliance to the proletarian
school of writers during the thirties and called White Folks the
"outstanding indictment of Nordicism in Modern American Fiction."
Only a year later John W. Parker (1949.B4), a prolific reviewer of
Hughes's works during the next ten years, repeated the cliche that
Carl Van Vechten called Hughes the Negro Poet Laureate and believed
that Hughes best represented the New Negroes. Of the negative reviewers, Harvey Curtis Webster stood out by saying that scholars had
neglected Hughes's works, writings so far "removed from the dominant
school of criticism." Yet--paradoxically--reflecting the aesthetic
values of this school, Webster criticized Hughes for expressing the
group rather than the individual.

Most criticism of the forties focused less on history than on the
man. Verna Arvey (1940.B1) portrayed a kind person who gave poems
away to Black editors. Arna Bontemps (1940.B2) described Hughes
on a Haitian journey, a "great lover of simple people." Edwin A.
Embree presented a left-wing Hughes who was free of "any church,
even the party's." In Negro Caravan (1941.B1) Sterling Brown and
Arthur P. Davis, two respected Black scholars, pictured Hughes the
cosmopolitan meeting many people in Africa, Asia, Europe, and America.
Thomas Yoseloff O'Sheel (1944.B2) also commended Hughes's universality and dedication to Blacks. When describing Hughes's open-
mindedness and humility, Rebecca Chalmer Barton depicted him as a
social mingler with people such as Rebecca West, Alfred Knopf, Louis
Untermeyer, Hugh Walpole, Jasha Heifetz, Salvador Dali, and Rudolph
Valentino. Hughes, according to Barton, loved the truth, and finally
Stella Kamp (1946.B1) characterized a mature Hughes who helped younger
writers and advised them to give their work away at first. With
Hughes in the forties, as with Brooks in the sixties and seventies,
the image of the human being existed clearly in the secondary works.

Some scholars, however, did emphasize the man less than his creations. Reviewing One-Way Ticket (1948.B3), fellow poet Melvin B.
Tolson stated that Hughes retained the touch of Weary Blues and portrayed the urban Negro as Paul Laurence Dunbar did the rural. By now
this urban-rural distinction has become cliche (see also 1976.B4),
even though Hughes occasionally created the tone and feel of Black
Southern dialect. To G. Lewis Chandler, Hughes was a synedochist
who used the racial as a means to the universal, an insight that
probably came from a subconscious belief in négritude or the idea
that fulfilling personal and racial identity is a means to achieving

a general humanity. By seeing no dichotomy between Black man and
Man, Chandler surpassed his contemporaries and many critics today.

Further writings discussed The Big Sea (1940), Shakespeare in
Harlem (1942), Fields of Wonder (1947) and One-Way Ticket (1949).
Theophilus Lewis's evaluation of the first has become questionable
in the seventies. The book, he said, presented no men or women of
stature; it portrayed, instead, only the near great, the shabby, and
the picturesque. Would one place W. E. B. DuBois, Alain Locke, and
Zora Neal Hurston--all who appear--in this latter category now? In
a second review (1940.B4) Milton Rugoff examined Hughes's self-image,
which he said was tolerant and naive. By contrast, Oswald Villard
(1940.B5) appreciated Hughes's portrait as being honest, frank, and
objective. Because Hughes lacked self-pity, The Big Sea, for Villard,
was an important document in the annals of American freedom.

Of major significance in the forties was Richard Wright's review
of The Big Sea, for here one read about Hughes's influence on Black
American letters. Hughes, according to Wright, made two major contributions. He freed Black literature from timidity as Theodore Dreiser
freed American letters from puritanism, and he became the ambassador
of a race. Wright's perception applied not merely to the Renaissance
of the twenties but to the wider patterns of a Black literature still
to emerge. Final reviews by Edwin Embree (1944.B3) and by
Henrietta L. Herod stressed form and content rather than Wright's
historical view. Embree conceded that the work was beautifully
written, even if it lacked spiritual depth or the question of caste
and class. Did the scene that portrayed Washington society's humilia-
tion of Carrie Hughes, Langston's mother, however, ignore class? Did
Hughes's final--but firm--separation from his patron exonerate even
the benevolently rich? To any of these questions, "yes" is too simple an answer. A thorough examination, rather, leads one to analyse
characterization and social theme simultaneously, as few reviewers
did.

So scholarship of the forties often repeated that of the twenties
and thirties. The forties, however, did offer at least two analyses
of style. An anonymous reviewer for Nation (1942.B1) recognized the
blues mood and the light tone of Shakespeare in Harlem; M. Column
(1952.B2) mentioned Hughes's strong emotion or the vocabulary of the
Blues and spirituals. These observations showed a concern for the
Black folk tradition and the cultural readings that would later characterize critics such as George Kent. Note Owen Dodson's remarks
(1942.B3), which also anticipated some others. Having pointed out
that Shakespeare had a superior format, Dodson called the work a
careless surface job unworthy of Hughes: He [Hughes] "is backing
into the future, looking at the past." This opinion was important
because Hughes was already shifting his interest from poetry to prose
and would never write another volume of verse as deep or lasting as
Weary Blues. The character Semple would occupy his time or possibly
the social essays would. By the publication of Panther and the Lash

(1967), his last book, Hughes would be a tired (if unbeaten) man re-
asserting his youthful vision. Dodson's insight stood out because it
came many years before anyone else noticed this change.

Often repetitious, other remarks during the forties were nevertheless diverse. H. R. Hays (1942.B4) discussed lightness and originality of style. Applying folk-cultural analysis, Alfred Kreymborg
(1942.B5) related Hughes to vaudeville musicians such as Bert Williams
and Eddie Leonard. Later Herbert Creekmore (1947.B2) described the
leanness, regionalism, and monotony of Hughes's work. Of the voices
during that decade, however, Rolfe Humphries's deserved particular
scrutiny. Because his scholarship would come to concern both Brooks
and Hughes--at varying times--his opposite ways of seeing these two
would show his personal preference and possibly that of the age. For
him Hughes and Brooks represented different manners. The first was
an innovator, but the second was a traditionalist. Humphries's comments made clear the cultural and temporal subjectivity of criticism.
In Hughes's verse, he wanted the following: more of the individual
and less of the racial spokesman; complex style; exploitation of education, travel, reading; and, finally, music other than the Blues.
Could Hughes, in short, be modern and white? As we shall see,
Humphries was kinder to Brooks. Yet the cultural insensitivity shown
here explains why he can describe her style but rarely convey her
meaning.

During the 1950's Hughes received serious attention. Because the
scholarship of that decade covered a wide range of creative books,
one cannot discuss here all of the relevant works. Consider Hughes's
variety during the period: Tambourines to Glory (hereafter Tambourines), comic novel; Semple Speaks His Mind (hereafter Semple Speaks),
comic tales; Montage of a Dream Deferred (hereafter Montage), jazz
poetry; Laughing to Keep from Crying (hereafter Laughing), short fiction; First Book of Negroes in America, chronology and history; I
Wonder as I Wander (hereafter Wonder), autobiography; Selected Poems
or collected verse. During this period--probably Hughes's most pro-
ductive--major scholars were John W. Parker and Arthur P. Davis.
Davis's two important contributions in Phylon (1952.B5; 1954.B3),
began an interest that would characterize his next twenty years.
First he explained that Hughes used Harlem both as a place and symbol,
and that by portraying one ghetto Hughes described all. Davis examined next the comic appeal of Semple, and later (1955.B4) discussed
the function of the tragic mulatto theme in Hughes's canon.

Parker reviewed books almost as swiftly as Hughes published them.
From an evaluation of Montage (1951.B4), he went on to analyse Laughing (1952.B9), and to present first his constant motif that Hughes's
effectiveness depends upon blending a humor of characterization with
a humor of situation. In reviewing First Book of Jazz (1955.B9)
(long before Donald C. Dickinson in the sixties and seventies),
Parker noticed Hughes's change of emphasis from poetry to prose.
Later he noticed the unity of action in Semple Stakes a Claim

(1957.B7) and in Tambourines to Glory (1959.B8). He recognized, too, the vagueness of organization, as well as the weakness of chronology, in Selected Poems (1959.B9). Most significantly, Parker observed the functioning of Medias Res in Hughes's world, an insight that ultimately should lead to a reexamination both of Hughes's major writings and their conceptions of time.

Much scholarship of the fifties concerned the character Semple, who was and is many readers' favorite creation by Hughes. Several reviewers praised the humor: William Pfaff (1950.B3), Carl Van Vechten (1950.B6), G. Lewis Chandler (1951.B1), Arna Bontemps (1953.B3), and Gilbert Millstein (1957.B6). Most of these commended as well the unique raciality of these tales, as did William Gardner Smith (1950.B5) and Luther Jackson (1957.B5). By situating Semple in the comic tradition of Mr. Dooley, J. Saunders Redding (1950.B4) and Philip Bonosky (1959.B2) provided helpful background.

Scholarship about Laughing, Tambourines, and Selected Poems gave a sample of the secondary publications during the decade. Arna Bontemps, Hughes's friend, said that the Great Depression characterized the setting of Laughing. While emphasizing his characteristic approach, Bontemps used history to reveal the text rather than the other way around. Additional writers such as Stanley Cooperman (1952.B4) and August Meir (1952.B7) complimented the good insight of the volume, and Worth Tuttle Heeden (1952.B6) appreciated the diversity of those social classes portrayed. Despite a generally favorable impression, Bucklin Moon (1952.B8) expressed a significant misgiving that would become more pronounced through the years. Many of Hughes's stories, he contended, would not outlive their times. To him survival of Hughes's short fiction depended less on the recording of historical situation than on the emphasis of human qualities.

By following Moon's reasoning, one would assume that Tambourines, which is humorous, should have outlasted Laughing, which is historical. But success of technique as well as quality of thought were important variables. Laughing, on the contrary, had the final advantage because, as the reviewers implied, Tambourines was superficial. After first locating in Tambourines a simplicity of plot and character, Richard Long perceived a mastery of Black idiom (1959.B7). Keith Waterhouse thought that the story amused but that Negro hymns occurred too frequently (1959.B8). Arna Bontemps (1958.B3) described Tambourines as effortless and ribald, if serious, while Hortense D. Lloyd (1950.B2) appreciated it as being compelling, compact, and lucid. By contrast, Gilbert Millstein (1958.B6) suggested that the skill and engagement of this work did not raise it above the level of minor literature.

Most significant in the fifties was James Baldwin's review of Selected Poems, since it reinforced the opinion of Harry Potamkin in the twenties, but anticipated an observation by George Kent in the seventies. According to Baldwin, Hughes should have been more

selective because he did not translate blues into art. The power of
Hughes's verses came from folk culture per se rather than from an
intense and imaginative recreation. For Baldwin, Hughes's most
skillful lyrics were "sardonic asides" such as "Mother to Son" and
"Negro Mother," and Hughes's aesthetic vision frequently collapsed
into monotonous documentary.

Because Hughes died during the sixties, he became a bridge between generations. In national and international publications, white
as well as Black, his death brought sympathetic responses: Nation,
Newsweek, Crisis, Freedomways, Negro Digest, and Présence Africaîne.
These essays portrayed a man of high conscience whom writers fondly
remembered. On May 22, 1967 he died in Polyclinic Hospital in New
York City. His affection for the young and his imaginative pictures
of the folk masses survived. He was generous, and his work reflected
the Black quest for freedom in North America. By extending the racial to the universal, he demonstrated much humanity.

Some observers misread the man and his efforts while others did
not. For a column in Newsweek, an anonymous reviewer phrased the
title "The Death of Simple." This caption ironically belied the complexity and depth of the man whom it would have honored. Although
the writer celebrated Hughes's social involvement in the thirties and
sympathized with Hughes's being blacklisted in the forties, he made
two errors: first, that Hughes was born with rhythm (a stereotypical
assertion); second, that in the era of Watts and sweeping social
change Hughes was an anachronism. In reflecting on this first assertion, one should remember the young Hughes described in The Big Sea.
When elected as class poet, he informed his peers that some Blacks
lacked rhythm, this having been his humorous way of enlightening them
about stereotype. As for the second assertion (that Hughes became an
anachronism), writers such as Mari Evans and Ted Joans suggested
otherwise because they praised Hughes's influence on their careers
and lives. In scores of essays about him, Black writers and critics
almost never saw Hughes as contributing to the generation gap, but
several white critics did. The first group focused on the Black
spiritual bond that went deeper than historical change; the second,
on the contrary, inferred that the Black spiritual state automatically
reflected changes in the historical world. These views represented
opposite ways of comprehending reality. Did one perceive of the
Black self as being in flux with history? Or did one identify this
self as representing all that stood against traditional history?
The question, put otherwise, was whether one stressed mutability or
permanence.

As already implied, the most thoughtful comments on Hughes came
from fellow Black writers. Gwendolyn Brooks (1967.B8) remembered his
inspiration to the young and his folk verisimilitude. Mari Evans
called him the "most generous professional I have ever known." Nicolas
Guillen (1978.B18) thought about Hughes's contribution to Black literature, and Arna Bontemps (1978.B1) recalled Hughes self-fidelity and

pattern of continuity. Most noteworthy, perhaps, was an observation
by Lofton Mitchell, a fine dramatist who said (perhaps too charitably?)
that Hughes was a greater man than he would ever become.

If, for Hughes, the sixties were a period of definitive work, one
reason was probably the emergence of James Emanuel, the most productive scholar on him to date. From an original analysis of Hughes's
first short story (1961.B2), Emanuel went on to an informative doctoral dissertation (1966.B2). En route he illuminated significant
areas: sixty-five short stories (1966.B2 and 1968.B9); biography
and négritude (1967.A1; 1967.B12); "Body in the Moonlight," the first
short narrative (1961.B2); Panther and the Lash (1968.B8). In Dark
Symphony, an anthology, Emanuel's brief biography of Hughes summarized
much knowledge gathered through seven years of intense research and
publication. Of the remaining scholars, Donald C. Dickinson and
W. Edward Farrison warrant attention. Both used a biographical or
historical approach. Although Dickinson's work, A Bio-Bibliography
of Langston Hughes (1964.A1; 1965.B1), was extensive, Farrison's
analyses were primarily reviews. With thorough homework Dickinson
traced Hughes's styles and themes back to the Brownie's Book, a children's publication of Crisis. Farrison's comments were more far-
reaching because they left few areas unexplored: Semple and his
comic tradition (1965.B2); Hughes's renown (1967.B14); Hughes's ex-
panding canon (1967.B15); Hughes's work in press at his death
(1968.B11); Hughes's revelation of the theme of American democracy
(1969.B4). With the same persistency that John Parker displayed in
the fifties, Farrison reviewed Hughes's work during the sixties. The
latter's productivity paralleled the growth and middle years of CLA
Journal (1957-   ). Like Therman B. O'Daniel, editor of this periodical, Farrison was a fellow student of Hughes at Lincoln University
in Pennsylvania.

In contrast with the Marxists of the thirties, the Farrison School
argued that Hughes believed in the American Dream. Editors such as
Faith Berry, by contrast, would bring back the Marxist tradition in
the seventies by insisting that Hughes was a revolutionary. Meanwhile Southern white critics such as James Presley would support
the Farrison School. So the sixties anticipated the seventies in
that both camps oversimplified. If Berry's edition and Hughes's
Panther (1967) showed a Marxist tone, the verse "Daybreak in Alabama,"
which appeared at the end of Hughes's final volume, restored Hughes's
apocalyptic dream. Hughes therefore emphasized (at least in the long
run) neither violent revolution nor American ideal; he illuminated
instead a paradoxical vision embracing both. Constantly resisting
each other, the two states coexisted for him less in harmony than in
nearly insoluble tension.

The seventies have shown a flowering of scholarship. Donald B.
Gibson's Five Black Writers (1970.B3) reprints one of Arthur P.
Davis's articles (1955.B4), as does Therman B. O'Daniel's Langston
Hughes: Black Genius (1971.A2). O'Daniel, however, used a different

essay (1968.B4). Davis's own <u>Dark Tower</u> (1974.B4) summarizes many of his insights about Hughes's work during a long and successful career. Since the sixties James Emanuel has continued to publish articles, and O'Daniel reprints Emanuel's condensed study of Hughes's short fiction (1968.B9). In Gibson's <u>Modern Black Poets: Twentieth Century Views</u>, Emanuel also discusses Langston Hughes's theme of religion. Two of Farrison's articles, one about <u>Not Without Laughter</u> and another about Hughes in the Harlem Renaissance, demonstrate the historical and literal approaches that have characterized his writing. Onwuchekwa Jemie's <u>Langston Hughes: An Introduction to the Poetry</u> maintains the Marxist method that has challenged the historical, cultural, and formalistic ones.

Of the younger critics, R. Baxter Miller has been productive. His first article (1975.B1), written about Hughes's women personae, focuses and reworks parts of his M.A. thesis (Brown University, 1972). Later he calls "Daybreak in Alabama" a resolution to Hughes's commentary on art and notes some contrasts between Hughes and Sterling Brown. Finally he proposes "home" as the unifying metaphor of <u>Not Without Laughter</u> (1976.B2) and attempts to combine the cultural approach of George Kent with the more formal method of Arthur Davis. Having profited from the historical background provided by Bontemps, Farrison, and others, Miller has tried to extend Hughes criticism into the area of structure, metrics, imagery, and myth.

The remaining scholarship of the seventies can be grouped as topics: biography, Renaissance, characterization, and primary work. O'Daniel (1971.B15) paraphrases the biographical information easily available in <u>The Big Sea</u>. Biographies by Elizabeth Myers (1970.B1) and Charlemae Rollins (1970.B2) also contribute in this area. As a children's book, Alice Walker's <u>Langston Hughes</u> (1974.B1) condenses the most telling scenes of <u>The Big Sea</u> into fewer than fifty pages. Patricia E. Taylor (1972.B11) and Faith Berry (1976.B1) situate Hughes's life in the Harlem Renaissance. Regarding Hughes as a folk poet, George Kent has excelled (1971.B11), although Nancy B. McGhee (1971.B13) and Edward E. Waldron (1971.B18) warrant reading. Hughes's character Simple is as popular as in the sixties. Charles A. Watkins (1970.B8) and Eugenia W. Collier (1971.B3) debate whether Simple is an epic hero, and Harry L. Jones examines Simple's language. Phyllis R. Klotman analyses the narrative technique of the Simple tales, and James Presley (1973.B6) appreciates that Semple has endured. Although less abundant, scholarship on <u>Not Without Laughter</u> comes from two people other than Farrison: Johnine Brown Miller (1970.B7) and Roger Rosenblatt (1974.B4). Miller's reading is more apt than Rosenblatt's, since Rosenblatt has agreed with Robert Bone (1958.B1) that Sandy, Hughes's protagonist, illustrates a split between white materialism and Black joy. Miller, by contrast, says that Sandy synthesizes the qualities of the other characters in Hughes's story. Finally, Richard K. Barksdale's recent book, <u>Langston Hughes: The Poet and His Critics</u> (Chicago: American Library Association, 1977) has shown wit, maturity, and discernment in evaluating scholarship written on Hughes during forty-seven years.

III. GWENDOLYN BROOKS

Because Hughes's race was conspicuous in his works, critics had
to consider his writings in a cultural and human context; since
Gwendolyn Brooks was more concerned with classical technique, however, the tendency was to ignore her color. For Brooks the scholarship of the forties, therefore, began to indicate the limitations of
formalism.

Before the 1960's most scholarship written about her was descrip-
tive--as opposed to analytical or definitive--and that of the forties
was no exception. The many entries in newspapers, especially in The
Chicago Daily News or The Chicago Sun, had a local flavor and a little explication. Mainly these columns described Brooks's prizes and
her Guggenheim fellowships. Other writings were usally reviews. In
Kirkus (1945.B1) an anonymous author said that Brooks was gifted, pas-
sionate, and authentic. He described her imagery as being arresting.
Another critic (1945.B2) recognized a mixture between traditional
forms and folk poetry, or a freshness. A third (1945.B5) observed
the influence of Blues on Brooks's verse and Brooks's concern for the
urban community. Unlike numerous other writers, this last reviewer
provided Brooks's poetry with a cultural context. The same, of course,
was less true for Rolfe Humphries (1949.B3) to whom Street in Bronzeville indicated a "good book and real poet"--but only by its form:
colloquialism, quatrains, free verse, ballads, and sonnets.

As for Annie Allen (1949) descriptive commentary was even more
characteristic. In Booklist (1949.B2) an anonymous reviewer said
that Annie moved beyond Street. This advance, according to him,
occurred because Brooks's new expression was less identifiably "Negro,"
although the themes still concerned city people. A second writer
(1949.B3), found less technical competence in Annie than in Street,
but believed that Annie was interesting and refreshing. By favoring
Brooks's first volume (1945) over her Pulitzer prize-winning one
(1949), this last reviewer deserved attention. To him Street and
Annie represented different efforts. The first sought to dramatize
the life of urban Blacks while the second attempted to create epic.
By weighing Brooks's implicit intentions against her accomplishments,
this reviewer contradicted most white scholars who praised Annie
merely for its classical mythology. An unsigned review for New
Yorker (1949.B4), praised Brooks's sense of form in Annie, since
Brooks could make a sonnet as "tight as a bowstring." What did
these sonnets mean? For the San Francisco Chronicle (1949.B5), a
reviewer wrote that Annie would widen Brooks's reputation, and commended Brooks's lyrical concreteness. Yet the same question about
meaning went unanswered. Even Van Allen Bradley, a reviewer for
Chicago papers, and a Brooks devotee, occasionally implied that most
poems lack human significance. In making clear that Brooks had exceptional promise, Bradley added that Annie was a further measure of
her talent: keener imagery, shrewd and sure technique, economy of

phrase, imagery that is sharp, distinctive, and often startling. He
then warned that at times she came perilously close to "yoking art to
propaganda." Is this process really propaganda or the presentation
of social theme? How did one distinguish between these two? This
and similar pieces of criticism during the forties, provided few
solutions because Brooks's reviewers disregarded the importance of
motif.

Of the remaining critics during the decade, only Lee Kennedy
(1949.B8) gave Brooks's poetry a social and historical context.
First, he set Brooks against the background of Chicago writing since
Nelson Algren; second, he compared Brooks with Hughes. Rolfe
Humphries, by contrast, continued to provide no cultural framework
(1949.B7). He preferred Annie to Street because Annie lacked so much
self-consciousness that made "one a little uncomfortable" when reading the other book. This observation is questionable, indeed, because self-consciousness in the title poem of Annie probably surpassed
that of any verse in Street. Since Annie had the lower self-
consciousness, and race is less noticeable in Annie, one assumes that
Humphries means "race" instead of "self." If Humphries, however,
ignored the ethnic tone of Brooks's poetry, could his reader trust
him? Did the "one" in his quoted phrase (above) represent people in
general or him?

Although Hughes received both positive and negative criticism
during the fifties, Brooks came by little of either. Then she published infrequently but listed Maud Martha (1953), as well as Bronzeville Boys and Girls (1956). Because of its esotericism, Annie Allen
(1959) had not primarily addressed Blacks. For them her transition
from Street had been a regression, and her classical style inspired
little enthusiasm. These observations are less apparent from commentary than from the scarcity of scholarship in Black periodicals.
Yet the Brooks of the fifties neither conspicuously opposed the tradition of Black protest, as did the early Baldwin, nor finally--
ambivalently--reaffirmed the American dream as did the early (and
late?) Ellison. Her absence of a genuine constituency made for
neglect.

General comments concerned Brooks's awards or prizes and usually
appeared in secondary publications--especially newspapers--such as
Chicago Daily News, Chicago Sun-Times, and Chicago Tribune. Frequently pieces discussed her public attendances. One column (1950.B1)
related her winning the Eunice Tienjens Award for a group of poems in
Poetry, and a second (1950.B2) showed that she earned $500 for the
Pulitzer Prize. Brief biographies appeared in standard sources of
the time: Who's Who in Chicago and Illinois; Herman Dreer, American
Literature by Negro Authors; James G. Fleming and Christian E. Bureke,
Who's Who in Colored America; Max J. Herzberg, The Reader's Enclope-
dia of American Literature. For other opinions about Brooks in the
fifties, one had to read brief reviews because no major essays
appeared. Two critiques concerning Annie, an anonymous one in

Introduction

United States Quarterly Books (1950.B10) and another by Babette
Deutsch (1950.B15), repeated many comments about style. Having
placed Brooks within the context of Black American culture, Deutsch
said that Brooks failed to utilize "Negro materials" fully. Deutsch,
however, never explained why or how. Elsewhere Phyllis McGinley
(1950.B2) criticized "Those little booths at Benevenuit's," where,
she said, Brooks became a "clever if somewhat trite social critic."
If the motif of this poem, however, is that people are human and universal despite racial color or geographical location, how was this
trite? McGinley complimented Annie Allen for its insight, wisdom,
and pity, but used no sound explication to demonstrate these qualities. Finally she warned Brooks to forget her [Brooks's] social
conscience and Guggenheim fellowships. McGinley was therefore so
charitable as to liberate Brooks from the sense of morality that made
Chaucer, Milton, and Dostoyevski great. Elsewhere Langston Hughes
(1950.B20) thought Annie was less direct and simple than Street but
found meaning and underlying structure: the progression from child-
hood to an age of love, and then the movement from this love to
motherhood.

Concerning Maud Martha and Bronzeville Boys and Girls (hereafter
Boys and Girls) the major commentors were still descriptive: an
unsigned writer for Kirkus (1953.B2); Van Allen Bradley (1953.B5);
Fanny Butcher (1953.B6); Herman Hogan (1953.B7); Nicholas Monjo
(1953.B8); and Coleman Rosenberger (1953.B10). When mentioning
Brooks's treatment of racial subjects, Butcher differed from the
rest, and Rosenberger stood out by noting that "novel" was an impre-
cise term for Maud Martha, a book that was a portrait and mosaic.
Meanwhile the scholarship written on Boys and Girls constantly
asserted Brooks's universality. Unnamed reviewers for New York
Herald Tribune Books (1956.B3) and Booklist (1956.B8), as well as
Margaret Sherwood Libby (1956.B8), appreciated the common appeal of
Boys and Girls. So the scholarship of the fifties showed again that
universality often concerned the literary work less than the critics'
perceptions. By the 1960's Hughes was already a subject for debate,
but Brooks's readers were just beginning to observe the cultural and
human significance of her work. Close readings of her poetry were
still conspicuously absent, although bibliographical and biographical
information provide useful foundation for future study. Contemporary
Authors (1962.B6) listed Brooks's primary works up to Bean Eaters, and
Russell L. Adams's Great Negroes Past and Present (1963.B9) summarized
her life. The Negro in American Literature, Bibliography by and About
Negro Americans (1966.B2) and Elizabeth Miller's checklist (1966.B3)
recorded the primary works up to Selected Poems (1963) while the
former also designated works by genre. Edgar A. Toppin, a general
biographer, wrote one of the most telling descriptions of Brooks's
verse, which to him "brilliantly evoked northern ghetto life and
universalized human experience in contemporary garb."

If the criticism of the forties revealed Hughes the man, the
scholarship of the sixties illuminated Brooks the woman. An unsigned

author pictured her as creating slowly or carefully and as showing
compassion. Carl Morse (1963.B19) said that she presented a warm
heart and cool head. Dorothy Witte Austin's interview portrayed a
woman with humility and candor. Conrad Kent Rivers (1964.B28)
described Brooks as a prophet and a disciple of truth.

The reviewers of Brooks's volume published during the sixties
discussed her style, development, and social concern. While looking
favorably upon her ballads, Geoffrey Hartman saw problems in a manner
that was folksy and sophisticated as well as runaway. Leonard E.
Nathan commented similarly on an approach that was elliptical, private, and obscure. Resembling these others, M. L. Rosenthal (1969.B10)
viewed Brooks's style as being overwrought with effects such as allit-
eration and internal rhymes as well as whimsicalness. Nick Aaron Ford
acknowledged Brooks's sense of irony and paradox (1961.B4), but noted
an absence of warmth. John Duffy (1963.B15) praised Brooks's control.

Few critics of the time, however, addressed themselves directly
to the two developments that colored their observations: first,
Brooks's evolution from classical forms to experimentations with free
verse and second, her greater concern with social themes. Some questions should have come up. Did her social motifs emerge only then?
Did the social focus of the decade, rather, change the readers or
reviewers so that they perceived her motifs? The evidence points to
the latter. Street in Bronzeville revealed the folk boldness and
flair of Black urban life, but reviewers commented on the success of
Brooks's ballads or sonnets as forms. · By 1960 one reviewer of Bean
Eaters (1960.B4) thought that Brooks's glibness and smugness undermined her idea. His reaction applied particularly to the tone of
"The CHICAGO DEFENDER Sends a Man to Little Rock," a verse about
school integration in 1957. Yet Brooks employs whimsicalness there
to support her irony and theme that civilization is as thin as those
social smiles that hide human barbarism. The reporter she portrays
finds that the inhabitants of this city are "like people everywhere"
while the context gives new meaning to this quoted phrase. The
reader had heard this saying before. It came perhaps with a tone of
clumsiness or the familiarity that allows one confidently to face
new situations and individuals. For Brooks's persona, however, this
awareness is not consoling but dreadful. By setting cliche within a
Black American perspective, she illuminates well its inherent irony
and pessimism. When Harvey Shapiro (1960.B10) concluded that
"Little Rock" was trite and the reader simple, one might have won-
dered how.

By 1963 writers provided Brooks's work with the kind of cultural
context that they had always given Hughes's. Consider Louis Simpson's
notorious remark that Brooks's writing was unimportant, if being a
Negro was the only subject, and one should criticize Brooks into
writing more poems such as "Bean Eaters." Robert S. Spector saw
much that Simpson missed: that tenderness underlay Brooks's indignation at racism while the anger and sympathy of her verse went deeper

than color. Here Spector repeated a reviewer's opinion of <u>Selected Poems</u> (1963.B8) and showed well the universality of Black American literature. For <u>Virginia Quarterly</u> an unsigned reviewer observed Brooks's self-consciousness as a Black and her sermon of life in the face of despair. Leonard G. Bird interpreted <u>Mecca</u> as being a micro-cosm of both the Black and human communities, and Dudley Randall (1969.B9) recorded Brooks's association with militant young writers in her workshop on the Chicago South-Side. For Randall Brooks would become not only a critic and fellow poet but a supportive admirer and friend. After <u>Mecca</u> she would shift her allegiance from Harper and Row, a prestigious white publisher, to Broadside, the leading Black press in America. But even Randall, the senior editor at Broadside, hardly implied that she was provincial.

In the seventies Brooks has become a literary and cultural symbol, as Hughes was in the sixties. But Hughes died in that decade. Except for an occasional breakthrough, Ralph Ellison, another major writer, has been silent for over two decades. Having grown into prominence during the early sixties, LeRoi Jones (Imamu Baraka) fades into Neo-Marxism and literary silence. For many Black Americans, Baldwin will always remain the talented expatriate, his accommodation of the fifties contradicting his rhetorical militancy of the seven-ties. All the while Brooks has kept publishing and renewed her vision or spirit.

Although Hughes has several critics during the seventies, Brooks has to rely on George Kent and William Hansel. By placing Brooks in the historical perspective of T. S. Eliot and Ezra Pound, Kent ably explains the characteristics of her style: irony, complexity, con-densation, and universality. If Kent is a major Black critic of long standing, Hansell is a white scholar who is relatively new. Within four years, however, the latter has published at least five papers. In his dissertation (1972.B4) he places Brooks within the tradition of Claude McKay, Countee Cullen, and Langston Hughes. Next (1973.B3) he differentiates between "The Chicago Picasso," which according to him indicates that art is self-justifying, and "The Wall," which im-plies the opposite. Third, Hansell asserts that Brooks's emphasis on Black identity and communal relationships separates poems after <u>Mecca</u> from those before, and then he states that <u>Riot</u> extends <u>Mecca</u>, since both works attempt to portray the "cause and significance of violence." Finally, Hansell says that <u>Family Pictures</u>, like <u>Beckonings</u>, resem-bles Brooks's verses of the late sixties (1976.B1).

Does Hansell miss the pervasive irony of "Chicago Picasso"? Is Brooks's theme that art is self-justifying or that traditional crit-ics err in thinking so? When suggesting that Brooks's style under-goes a significant change, Hansell resembles the militant poet Don L. Lee (Haki Madhubuti, 1972.B2; 1972.B8) more than George Kent or Toni Cade Bombara (1973.B2). Through her personae—as Kent and Bombara know—Brooks has almost always revealed the Black community and changes in her style must be of degree rather than kind. Comparing

"Sadie and Maud" (<u>Street</u>) with the title poem of <u>Mecca</u> justifies the
contentions of these latter two writers. In "Sadie," one persona, a
liberated woman, breaks with social rules and lives her own life.
Thirteen years later Mrs. Sallie Smith of <u>Mecca</u> seeks her dead child,
Pepitia, inside a ghetto tenement while other dwellers reflect and
intensify this mother's grief. But in both poems the theme is human
quest. If Hansell and Lee have focused on Brooks's plots and characters that change, Kent and Bombara have stressed Brooks's continuous
and deeper patterns of consciousness as well as her social insight.
Other scholarship of the seventies comes from two women. While dis-
cussing Brooks's literary growth or development, Annette Oliver Shands
(1973.B10) has contributed the only essay on <u>Maud Martha</u>, Brooks's
autobiographical novel, and Gloria Hull (1975.B1) has analysed
Brooks's syntax and economy of words. For these and other scholars,
standard reference works are now accessible: David Ray's <u>Contemporary
Poets of the English Language</u> (1970.B6), which lists Brooks's primary
works and anthologies up to 1968, and James M. McPherson's <u>12 Blacks
in America</u>, which makes similar listings.

IV. INSIGHT AND THE FINAL UNITY

So a half-century after Locke and DuBois wrote about Hughes and
the Harlem Renaissance, Kent and Hansell begin to show the richness
and complexity of Brooks's verse. Although the careers of Hughes
and Brooks intersected by twenty-two years, their different tempera-
ments grew out of separate times. Hughes, again, maintained a romantic vision because he experienced the Marxist thirties and matured
before World War I. While still young, Brooks faced the paradox of
the world after the war. Brooks's imagination has held only a slight
advantage on chaos but still conceives of love. Her verse, often a
microcosm of human evolution, shows a ironic stress between good and
evil. Finally her force, paradoxically, comes from the suggestion
of frailty or vulnerability.

Such observations appear only recently. In the 1940's writers
overlooked Hughes innovations in form, but overemphasized Brooks's
technique, and by the 1950's Hughes already had an audience, although
Brooks needed hers. During the sixties, scholars saw these two
authors--withstanding their different sensibilities--as those who
most capably adapted to a period of sit-ins and a disillusioning
white backlash. For Hughes the seventies have been a time of scholarly study and posthumous remembrance. Brooks, however, is still
at her best.

V. FORMULATION AND PROCEDURE

Some general comments about the method and scope of this work
may prove helpful. In compiling this bibliography, I have relied

on the following sources: <u>Essays and General Literature Index</u>, <u>Selected Periodicals By and About Negroes</u>, <u>Biography Index</u>, <u>Reader's Guide to Periodical Literature Book Reviews in the Humanities</u>, <u>MLA Bibliography</u>, <u>Bibliography of English Language and Literature</u>, <u>Book Review Digest</u>, and <u>New York Times Index</u>. In regard to Brooks, I have used Jon Loff's helpful bibliography (1973.B6) and have occasionally corrected Loff's entries when they are misprinted or incomplete. Where references are to Chicago newspapers, page numbers are absent because the clippings are available only from the morgues. Unlocatable items are indicated by an asterisk. As for annotations, the point of view is usually the original author's, although bibliographical essays are exceptions. Throughout I seek to maintain an author's diction whenever possible. Sometimes the annotations are unclear because their authors are; in other instances, entries become bumpy in my attempts to approximate the initial tone. Where pieces are highly verbose, however, I try to rephrase for condensation and accuracy. Since an all-inclusive book, as this, annotates racist and inhumane comments as well as truthful ones, the serious student should read different points of view and question the trustworthiness of all narrators.

This volume makes clear some areas for future research. Hughes scholars have exhausted most discussion about the Harlem Renaissance; similarly, little remains to be said either about Simple or the American Dream. Although critics have written about blues or jazz, they can press further to show that music, for Hughes, represents a mental victory over death and reasserts hope or faith. Opportunity remains to analyse individual volumes such as <u>Fields of Wonder</u>, <u>One-Way Ticket</u>, or--especially--<u>Ask Your Mama</u>. One might write about the function of Nature in Hughes's verse; or, by juxtaposing <u>The Big Sea</u> with the <u>Education of Henry Adams</u>, might explain each work as well as characterize American society. Because Hughes is often taken to be a simple writer, his deceptive complexity and impressive irony remain relatively unexplored. Despite O'Daniel's edition, one awaits a definitive text of the kind. While this collection contains writings by many scholars--most are members of the College Language Association--it needs a greater diversity of contributors. Most helpful would be adding commentary by creative writers Gwendolyn Brooks, James Baldwin, Owen Dodson, and Loften Mitchell. White scholars such as Robert Bone and Kenneth Kinnamon have made debatable points at times, but they have an audience, and any definitive collection should include their work.

Opportunities to write about Gwendolyn Brooks abound, especially since the disproportion of this study reflects the imbalance of scholarship written about her and Hughes. Surpassing him in the mastery of craft, Brooks has fewer than ten perceptive essays written about her work. One should discuss the irony in her sonnets or the theme of truth in her ballads and the way that her various forms such as the rhyme royal skillfully present her social meaning.

Except for <u>Mecca</u>, all of her volumes still need independent evaluation, and of particular significance would be studies on her charac-
terizations, experimentations with epic form, and narrative voices.
Analysing the development of her style through different personae
would also be valuable. In certain areas Hughes criticism is already
redundant, although Brooks scholarship is still uncharted. The
secondary works in the future, like the ablest in the past, should
show the different skills by which these authors portray that Blacks
are human and universal.

<u>Note</u>--Please note that two spellings are in common usage for one of
Hughes's characters: these are Simple and Semple.

Acknowledgments

For the completion of this work, I am indebted to numerous individuals and institutions. To many I owe gratitude for their general suggestions and for their influence on my thoughts in the subject area: George E. Kent, Richard K. Barksdale, Houston A. Baker, Jr., Ronald Gottesman, Michael S. Harper, and Charles H. Nichols. To others I am grateful for the assistance in searching materials and for the help in organizing a process to locate them: Bjorg Miehle and the staff of the James P. Magill Library, Patricia Wright, and Marie Ashton. As my research assistant for the summer of 1975, Ms. Ashton did an excellent job. Without her hard work, this book would have taken several months more. Throughout the two and a half years of research, the libraries of many institutions have been prompt and kind: Wisconsin State University, Stevens Point; Wisconsin Education Association Council; Villanova University; Pennsylvania State University; Brown University; University of Pennsylvania; Haverford, Bryn Mawr, and Swarthmore colleges. To some independent institutions, I also express appreciation: Free Library of Philadelphia; Harper and Row; Broadside Press; <u>Chicago Daily News</u> and <u>Chicago Sun Times</u>; Schomburg Collection; and National Endowment for the Humanities. For the typing of correspondences or parts of the manuscript, I thank Linda Corwin, Patricia Wright and, especially, Mildred Hargreaves. Jessica G. Miller kindly read the proofs, and Aaron L. Fessler cooperated by doing the indexing. To Haverford College I owe special appreciation, since two of its research grants supported me in the contracting for professional services. My gratitude to the National Endowment concerns a summer grant for 1975. This period of study was invaluable in the researching of essays that helped to prepare for the project. During the tenure of that award, the study began in full. I thank no less the persons who recommended my form of application: James D. Boulger, George P. Landow, John Ashmead, and Charles Nichols. Although I decided not to focus on primary works in my introduction, both Harper and Broadside gave me permission to quote from Brooks's works. The latter was particularly generous and encouraging, and both publishers contributed free books. To those named above goes much of the credit for the production of this volume, but I am responsible for all the faults.

Journal Abbreviations

AM	American Mercury
AtlM	Atlantic Monthly
Ban	Bancroftiana
BALF	Black American Literature Forum (formerly Negro American Literature Forum)
Black W	Black World
CA	Chicago American
CC	Christian Century
CDD	Chicago Daily Defender
CDN	Chicago Daily News
CEA	CEA Critic
CE	College English
CLAJ	College Language Association Journal
CMBST	Chicago Magazine of Books: Sunday Tribune
COS	Cleveland Open Shelf
Crisis	The Crisis
CS	Chicago Sun
CSM	Christian Science Monitor
CST	Chicago Sun Times
CT	Chicago Tribune
DA	Dissertation Abstracts
DC	The Drama Critique
Hor	Hornbook
InL	International Literature (later becomes Soviet Literature)
JML	Journal of Modern Literature
JNL	Journal of Narrative Technique

Kan Q	Kansas Quarterly
KCS	Kansas City Star
KeR	Kenyon Review
KiR	Kirkus Reviews
LJ	Library Journal
LUB	Lincoln University Bulletin
MaM	Masses and Mainstream
MidJ	Midwest Journal
MJ	Milwaukee Journal
MR	Massachusetts Review
NALF	Negro American Literature Forum (later becomes BALF)
NAR	North American Review
ND	Negro Digest
NER	Negro Educational Review
NHB	Negro History Bulletin
NM	New Masses
NR	New Republic
NS	New Statesman
NYAN	New York Amsterdam News
NYHT	New York Herald Tribune
NYHTB	New York Herald Tribune Books
NYHTBR	New York Herald Tribune Book Review
NYT	New York Times
NYTBR	New York Times Book Review
PA	Présence Afrîcaine
PP	Pittsburgh Press
PW	Publisher's Weekly
Rblp	Revue bleue littéraire et politique
RJT	Racine Journal Times
R&W	Readers & Writers
SatR	Saturday Review
SBL	Studies in Black Literature
SFC	San Francisco Chronicle
SG	Survey Graphic
SJ	Southwest Journal

SN	Satire Newsletter
SoR	Southern Review
SWR	Southwest Review
USQB	US Quarterly Book List
VQR	Virginia Quarterly Review
WLB	Wilson Library Bulletin
WLJ	Wisconsin Library Journal
XVS	Xavier University Studies

Langston Hughes

Major Writings by Langston Hughes

The Weary Blues, 1926

Fine Clothes to the Jew, 1927

Not Without Laughter, 1930

Dear Lovely Death, 1931

The Negro Mother, 1931

The Dream Keeper and Other Poems, 1932

Scottsboro Limited, Four Poems and a Play in Verse, 1932

Popo and Fifina, Children of Haiti, 1932

The Ways of White Folks, 1934

Troubled Island (libretto), 1935

A New Song, 1938

Don't You Want to Be Free, 1938

The Big Sea, 1940

Shakespeare in Harlem, 1942

Freedom's Plow, 1943

Jim Crow's Last Stand, 1943

I Hear America Singing: Selected Poems of Walt Whitman, 1946

Fields of Wonder, 1947

Masters of the Dew, 1947

Cuba Libre (translated), 1948

Street Scene (lyrics), 1948

One Way Ticket, 1949

The Poetry of the Negro, 1946-1949, 1949

Tambourines to Glory, 1950

Simple Speaks His Mind, 1950

Voices (edited); Quarterly of Poetry: Negro Poets Issue, Winter, 1950

Prelude to Our Age, October, 1950

Gypsy Ballads, 1951

Montage of a Dream Deferred, 1951

Laughing to Keep from Crying, 1952

The First Book of Negroes, 1952

Simple Takes a Wife, 1953

Lincoln University Poets, 1954

Famous American Negroes, 1954

The First Book of Rhythms, 1954

The First Book of Jazz, 1955

Famous Negro Music Makers, 1955

Sweet Flypaper of Life, 1955

Pictorial History of the Negro in America, 1956

I Wonder as I Wander, 1956

Simple Stakes a Claim, 1957

Tambourines to Glory: A Novel, 1958

The Langston Hughes Reader, 1958

The Book of Negro Folklore, 1958

Selected Poems of Langston Hughes, 1959

Simply Heavenly, 1959

The First Book of Africa, 1960

An African Treasury: Articles, Essays, Stories, Poems by Black Africans (edited), 1960

Ask Your Mama: 12 Moods for Jazz, 1961

The Best of Simple, 1961

Fight for Freedom: The Story of the NAACP, 1962

Five Plays by Langston Hughes, edited by Webster Smalley (Mulatto, Soul Gone Home, Little Ham, Simply Heavenly, and Tambourines to Glory), 1963

Poems from Black Africa (edited), 1963

Something in Common and Other Stories, 1963

New Negro Poets U.S.A. (edited), 1964

Simple's Uncle Sam, 1965

The Book of Negro Humor (edited), 1966

La Poésie Negro-Americaine; Anthology (edited), 1966

The Best Short Stories by Negro Writers, 1967

The Panther and the Lash: Poems of Our Times, 1967

Black Magic: A Pictorial History of the Negro in American
   Entertainment, 1967

Black Nativity and Mother to Child (uncollected)

Writings about
Langston Hughes, 1924-1977

1924 A BOOKS - NONE

1924 B SHORTER WRITINGS

   1   DU BOIS, W. E. B. "The Younger Literary Movement," Crisis,
        27 (February), 161-163.
            In Langston Hughes's "Song for a Banjo," we recognize
        the "exquisite abandon of a new day."

   2   KERLIN, ROBERT T. "A Pair of Youthful Negro Poets," SW
        (April), pp. 178-181.
            Hughes and Countee Cullen are "friends and kindred
        spirits," yet with individual and distinctive merits.
        Cullen relies on traditional ballad form and Hughes on
        free verse.

1925 A BOOKS - NONE

1925 B SHORTER WRITINGS

   1   LOCKE, ALAIN. The New Negro. New York: Charles Boni,
        pp. 4-5.
            Langston Hughes has a distinctive fervency of color and
        rhythm, and a biblical simplicity of speech that is col-
        loquial in derivation, but full of artistry.

1926 A BOOKS - NONE

1926 B SHORTER WRITINGS

   1   ANON. "Five Silhouettes on the Slope of Mount Parnassus,"
        NYTBR (March 21), pp. 6, 16.
            On The Weary Blues. A natural troubador, Hughes is the
        "most startling of all in the "advance guard from Parnassus."
        The publisher should have avoided putting the inferior work,
        the jazz poems, in the forefront of the book. Hughes's

1926

verses are superior to the jazz poetry that is peddled on
Broadway and "not inferior to Vachel Lindsay's." Hughes
"does not dwell upon the burden of race; he is too light-
hearted to be long cast down." Should he continue his
progress, "America bids fair to have a poet worthy of far
more than passing mention."

2   CULLEN, COUNTEE. "Poet on Poet," Opportunity, 4 (March 4),
73-74.
    On The Weary Blues. Hughes is a poet with whom to
reckon. He represents a "transcendently emancipated spirit
among a class of writers whose particular battle cry is
freedom." He is "scornful in subject matter, in photog-
raphy, and rhythmical treatment, of whatever obstructions
time and tradition have placed before him...it is essential
that he be himself." Had Hughes controlled himself better,
some of the poems would have been better. Can jazz poems
really belong to that "select and austere circle of high
literary expression which we call poetry"? The one-
sidedness of the selections tend to make Hughes one of
those Negro writers who "are racial artists instead of
artists pure and simple." Too much emphasis falls upon
strictly Negro themes.

3   FAUSET, JESSIE. "Our Book Shelf," Crisis, 30-31 (March), 239.
    On The Weary Blues. I took "The Negro Speaks of Rivers"
to Dr. Du Bois and asked "what colored person in the
United States could write this way and be unknown." That
Hughes is never preoccupied with form is not a fault
but a virtue, for his verse has a "perfection of spontaneity."
He achieves a remarkable objectivity for one so young, and
this is a first step toward philosophy. Hughes should write
more dialect poems. Perhaps no one else will ever write
as tenderly, understandingly, and humorously about the life
in Harlem. This and the sea are his great loves. His
verses are a brilliant and sensitive interpretation of
life's multiplicity.

4   HEYWARD, DU BOSE. "The Jazz Band's Sob," NYHT (Sunday,
August 1), p. 4.
    On The Weary Blues. Although only twenty-four, Hughes
is "already conspicuous in the group of Negro intellectuals
who are dignifying Harlem." He has done "nothing particularly revolutionary in the field of rhythm." Endowed with
too subtle a musical sense to use Vachel Lindsay's banjo
music, he can better be compared to Carl Sandburg in his
use of free and subtle syncopation. Amy Lowell might
have written several of the poems that are in free verse.

Hughes, however, has captured the essence of the Blues.
Occasionally the artist obscures the propagandist. Hughes's
first book begins a career that deserves to be watched.

5   LOCKE, ALAIN. "The Weary Blues," Palms, 1, No. 1, 25-27.
       Although these verses are pure poetry, they also repre-
    sent a race poet. Since Negro folk rhythms saturate his
    poetry, Hughes is a "people's poet." He has "their bal-
    ladry in his veins." If Dunbar was the "showman of the
    Negro masses," Hughes is their spokesman. The clean sim-
    plicity and absence of sentimentalism distinguish the work.

6   SERGEANT, ELIZABETH. "The New Negro," NR, 46 (May 12), 371-372.
       On The Weary Blues. Hughes is that youngest and freest
    and perhaps most happily gifted of Negro poetic adventures.
    Style is colloquial, casual, fervent--in the "manner of the
    race." The book "may well be an historic landmark."

1927 A BOOKS - NONE

1927 B SHORTER WRITINGS

1   ANON. "What to Read," Crisis (March), p. 20.
       On Fine Clothes to the Jew. Hughes's volume is the out-
    standing book of the month. Like The Weary Blues, Fine
    Clothes to the Jew has force, passion, directness and per-
    ception. Although confined to lowly types, the emphasis
    falls upon human feeling and longing.

2   DEUTSCH, BABETTE. "Four Poets," Bookman, 65 (April), 220.
       On Fine Clothes to the Jew. Completely unliterary,
    Hughes's verses are "often wilfully [sic] illiterate, and
    as naively vital as any old ballad or folk song." The
    dialect pieces "fairly sing themselves when read aloud";
    others show high craftsmanship.

3   FEARING, KENNETH. "Limiting Devices," NM, 3 (September), 29.
       On Fine Clothes to the Jew. Although the poems have a
    "certain amount of power and a great deal of ease," Hughes
    is yet unfamiliar with the American language. He has done
    more with his "conventional 'Negro stuff'...than...any
    other dialect writer."

4   GORMAN, HERBERT S. "Tradition and Experiment in Modern Poetry,"
    NYTBR (March 27), p. 2.
       On Fine Clothes to the Jew. Because Hughes is colored,
    it is impossible to compare him with Humbert Wolfe or

1927

Richard Addington. Hughes exemplifies the Negro renascence. Uneven and flawed, his book displays "flashes of authentic inspiration." The Blues poems are the best and give a "vivid sensation of the Negro spirit."

5   HEYWARD, DU BOSE. "Sing A Soothin' Song," NYHTB (Sunday, February 20), p. 5.
      With The Weary Blues, Hughes sounded a "new note in contemporary American poetry." Fine Clothes to the Jew is more even in quality but lacks the high spots of The Weary Blues and is less unforgettable. Although this volume does not elevate Hughes's verses to a new and high level, it "renews his high promise for the future."

6   LOCKE, ALAIN. "Common Clay and Poetry," SatR, 3 (April 9), 712.
      Stripping life down, but still poetizing it, Fine Clothes to the Jew is more starkly realistic and colloquial than The Weary Blues. The success of the poems depends on the clever and apt usage of "folksong forms and idioms." Blues is the dominant mood. The lyric "Mulatto" condenses the deepest tragedy of the race problem. "Song for a Dark Girl" also demonstrates social and individual tragedy.

7   _____. The Pamphlet Poets. New York: Simon and Schuster, pp. 5-6.
      By a "quite ecstatic sense of kinship with even the most common and lowly folk," Langston Hughes "discovers...in spite of their individual sordidness and backwardness, the epic quality of collective strength and beauty." Hughes is the Dunbar of his generation. He brings to the portrayal of his folk, however, "not the ragged provincialism of a minstrel but the descriptive detachment of a Vachel Lindsay and Sandburg and promises the democratic sweep and universality of a Whitman."

8   NILES, ABBE. "Real and Artificial Folk Song," NR, 51 (June 8), 77.
      On Fine Clothes to the Jew. Hughes's dialect verse is the most interesting part of the volume.

9   OVINGTON, MARY WHITE. Portraits in Color. Freeport: Books for Libraries, pp. 194-204.
      Hughes has been "much criticized by the intelligentsia of his race for not writing of them."

10   PETERKIN, JULIA. "Negro Blue and Gold," Poetry, 31 (1927-28), 44-47.

Fine Clothes to the Jew "interprets the emotions of
primitive types of American Negroes." Without using conventional forms, Hughes has created "the sign of an unfail-
ing musical sense." Hughes's art and skill allow all human
beings to experience comedy, tragedy, gaiety and despair.

11   POTAMKIN, HARRY ALAN. "Old Clothes," The Nation, 124
     (April 13), 403-404.
       Hughes is a Negro writer of a third category: those
     that recognize the need for a separate communication of
     racial material but whose aesthetic apprehension or control
     is not adequate. The other two groups concern those writers
     who have capitalized racial identity but have not studied
     it, and those who use the essential material for its recrea-
     tion under aesthetic suasion (Toomer only). Fine Clothes
     to the Jew does not progress beyond The Weary Blues, since
     one finds no evidence of Hughes's converting folk materials
     into art. One misses the personal idiom that makes sensa-
     tion new.

1929 A BOOKS - NONE

1929 B SHORTER WRITINGS

1   SCHOELL, F. L. "Un Poète Nègre," Rblp, 67 (July 20), 436-438.
       Although Black Americans have had their problems in the
     theater, they have some poets who "valent les meilleurs
     parmi ceux d'Amerique." Hughes is "un des plus dignes
     l'être connus en France." Of all adventurers, he is "celui
     qui a le plus périlleusement roulé 'sa bosse." Hughes's
     greatest virtues are "l'âme, des impossibles désirs et la
     mélancolie profonde des Négres ses frères."

1930 A BOOKS - NONE

1930 B SHORTER WRITINGS

1   ANON. "The Browsing Reader," Crisis, 37 (September), 321.
       Although being realistic, close to human beings, Not
     Without Laughter is a story of character rather than one
     of plot. Not strongly knit, it may not "hold the sustained
     interest of many readers." Well written, it ends in
     optimism.

2   BRICKELL, HERSCHEL. "A Poet's Debut as Novelist," SatR, 7
     (August 23), 69.

1930

"Tender understanding" distinguishes this volume from
most Negro fiction. Not Without Laughter is "subtly
simple...at times bordering on the biblical in the direct-
ness of its narrative." Hughes's "unflinching honesty" and
his creation of empathy make for strength.

3   CALVERTON, V. F.   Review of Not Without Laughter, The Nation,
      31 (August 6), 157-158.
        The novel has "that quick and intimate reality which is
      seldom seen in American fiction." It has defects of style
      and weakness of structure. The first half arrives at points
      of interest slowly; afterward the tempo picks up but there
      are no great situations or "high points of intensity"; nor
      is there rigor of style. Nevertheless, Not Without Laughter
      is significant despite its weaknesses because "even where
      it fails, it fails beautifully." It succeeds in intimate
      characterization, local color, and charm.

4   CARMON, WALT.   "From Harlem," NM, 6 (October), 17-18.
        Not Without Laughter is a "definite contribution to both
      Negro and proletarian literature in America." A first,
      it breaks with the tradition of Negro burlesque and vulgari-
      zation sponsored by Van Vechten. Although this break is
      not complete, it is far beyond Home to Harlem. Since
      Hughes reveals the bitterness of the Negro worker, race
      feeling beclouds issues of class. Because oppressors of
      Negroes are almost always white, the bitterness and hatred
      are misdirected at the white race as a whole. The book
      concludes without a point, but has "red proletarian blood."

5   JOHNSON, JAMES WELDON.   Black Manhattan.   New York: Alfred A.
      Knopf, pp. 271-273.
        Hughes is a rebel in content, as well as in form, and
      is as likely to take a subject from the gutter as from any-
      where else. This course has caused some consternation
      among Negroes who feel that his subjects are not suffi-
      ciently high. Yet Hughes's best work springs from the idea
      of race. He treats this with a cynicism and a "sardonic
      humor peculiarly his own." The effects differ from Cullen's
      but "have a quality of equal finality." Seldom being sen-
      timental, Hughes is never pathetic. His work is often off
      the surface, for he has "adopted the philosophy of the folk
      bards, makers of the blues. That philosophy consists in
      choosing to laugh to keep from crying."

6   REDDING, J. SAUNDERS.   To Make a Poet Black.   Chapel Hill:
      University of North Carolina Press, pp. 113-117.

Hughes is the most prolific and "most representative of
the New Negroes." At that end of poetry opposite from
Cullen, he realizes and expresses the "dark perturbation
of the soul." Hughes uses the Blues form and shout.
In "Negro Artist and the Racial Mountain," The Nation
(June 16, 1926), he described accurately the New Negro.

7   ROSS, MARY. "A Little Colored Boy Grows Up," NYHTBR (Sunday,
     July 27), p. 5.
          Hughes shows Negroes who are human beings. Because of
     its verisimilitude and fidelity to life, Not Without Laugh-
     ter should not be called "The Negro Novel." Philosophy
     occasionally takes over.

1932 A BOOKS - NONE

1932 B SHORTER WRITINGS

1   BENÉT, WILLIAM ROSE. "Round About Parnassus," SatR, 9
     (November 12), 241.
          The illustrations are excellent, and the best poems are
     in the third section. Hughes is not first rate, "even
     among those of his own race." But he is distinctly appeal-
     ing, a "melodist who touches with sensitiveness the stops
     of his black flute."

2   CALVERTON, V. F. The Liberation of American Literature.
     New York: Charles Scribners Sons, pp. 445-446.
          In Hughes's poetry, there is a freshness, even in arti-
     fice, which was absent in the poetry of individual Negro
     poets in the nineteenth century.

3   EATON, ANNE T. "The New Books for Children," NYTBR
     (July 17), p. 13.
          On The Dream Keeper and Other Poems. The group of
     verses called "Walk with the Dawn" gives the reader an
     imaginative understanding of the poet's feeling toward his
     own people. Helen Sewell's illustrations have "beauty" and
     an "unaffected simplicity" that suggest realism.

1933 A BOOKS - NONE

1933 B SHORTER WRITINGS

1   FILATOVA, LYDIA. "Langston Hughes: American Writer," InL,
     No. 1, pp. 103-105.

1934

        Hughes is one of the important poets of America today,
and so far is the only established Negro writer whose work
tends to leave the beaten track of petty bourgeois and
Negro literature. The Weary Blues placed Hughes near the
first rank of American poets. The lyrics are "among the
best examples of contemporary literature." Departing from
the canons of classic poetry, he was strangely influenced
by Walt Whitman and Carl Sandburg. Simplicity characterizes his poetry, and he excels in verse miniatures or grace-
ful cameos. Brevity and irony are the keys to his success.
The publication of Not Without Laughter was significant in
contemporary American literature. It marked an important
stage in Hughes's creative growth and in the development
of Negro literature. Breaking with the Harlem tradition,
Hughes becomes a realistic writer. He is the "first revolutionary poet of the Negro proletariat."

1934 A BOOKS - NONE

1934 B SHORTER WRITINGS

1   ANDERSON, SHERWOOD. "Paying for Old Sins," The Nation, 139
       (July 11), 49-50.
          On The Ways of White Folks. Although the Negroes are
       alive, warm, and real, the whites are caricatures, pre-
       tentious and fake. "Mr. Hughes, my hat is off to you in
       relation to your own race, but not to mine." Oceola Jones
       is the most finely drawn of characters, and the book is
       good.

2   BRICKELL, HERSCHEL. "The Literary Landscape," NAR, 238
       (September), 286.
          The Ways of White Folks contains "some of the best
       stories that have appeared in this country in years." The
       volume strengthens one's opinion that Hughes is the most
       talented Black American writer.

3   GREGORY, HORACE. "Genius of Langston Hughes," NYHTB (Sunday,
       July 1), p. 4.
          Hughes's work has kept pace with his growing reputation
       and with his early promise. The Ways of White Folks is
       race-conscious and class-conscious, but transcends docu-
       mentary literature. Hughes proves that the dichotomy be-
       tween art and propaganda is true only when the writer fails
       to make his work convincing. "Cora Unashamed" is one of
       the best stories. The book contains two remarkable pieces
       on lynching: "Home" and "Father to Son." Although the

devices are stock, Hughes contributes a "spiritual prose
style and an accurate understanding of human character...."
He reveals genius.

4   GRUENING, MARTHA. "White Folks are Silly," NR, 80
    (September 5), 108-109.
        The Ways of White Folks suffers from Hughes's perception
    that whites are "either sordid and cruel, or silly and
    sentimental." The best of these stories are "very good
    indeed." One searches to explain Hughes's reason for
    including satire or "A Good Job Gone."

*5 HOLMES, E. C. Opportunity (September), pp. 283-284.
        Unlocatable. Listed in Dickinson (1972.B1).

6   LOCKE, ALAIN. "Negro Angle," SG (November), p. 565.
        On The Ways of White Folks. The stories are "challenging
    to all who would understand the later phases of the race
    question." The "most illuminating moods" consist in tragic
    irony and caustic satire--"Father to Son" and "Cora Un-
    ashamed." This is an important book for the present times.
    Greater artistry, deeper sympathy, and less resentment would
    have made it a book for all times.

7   LOGGINS, VERNON. "Jazz Consciousness," SatR, 10 (July 14),
    805.
        Among present Negro authors, Hughes has been the most
    jazz-conscious. The Ways of White Folks is his strongest
    work. Hughes's literary talent combines cynicism, sarcasm,
    radicalism, and urbane humor.

8   STREATOR, GEORGE. "A Nigger Did It," Crisis, 41 (July), 216.
        Hughes laughs at white people of all social classes.
    Not all of the stories rise to the Hughes standard, and
    none is revolutionary in the sense that Hughes is being
    portrayed as being. There is a struggle between black and
    white, but no class struggle.

1937 A BOOKS - NONE

1937 B SHORTER WRITINGS

1   BROWN, STERLING. The Negro in American Fiction. Washington:
    Associates in Negro Folk Education, passim.
        Not Without Laughter is one of the best novels by a
    Negro author. Except Aunt Tempy, who is sharply satirized

1937

       as a high-tone striver, all of the characters are treated
with sympathy. Rendered with poetic realism, this is a
good novel about boyhood.

2   _____. Negro Poetry and Drama. Washington: The Associates
in Negro Folk Education.
      Hughes took the urban masses for his subject, and he
used them to create his own commentary on America.

1938 A BOOKS - NONE

1938 B SHORTER WRITINGS

1   MacLEOD, NORMAN. "The Poetry and Argument of Langston
Hughes," Crisis, 45 (November), 358-359.
      On Don't You Want to be Free. It lacks the emotional
appeal found in Clifford Odet's Waiting for Lefty, and lies
halfway between Marc Blitztein's Cradle Will Rock and Labor
Stage's production of Pins and Needles. Hughes continues
to widen the horizons of his first work. During the Harlem
Renaissance, he was probably unique and went his personal
way honestly and sincerely. A folk poet from the beginning,
he records this time and place. He "feels more than thinks,"
and the play is agi-prop [sic]. Although his empathy with
the Negro rings true, his empathy with members of the white
and black working classes is forced. The drama does not
measure up to his work as a whole.

1939 A BOOKS - NONE

1939 B SHORTER WRITINGS

*1   CARMEN, Y. "Langston Hughes: Poet of the People," InL, No. 1,
pp. 192-194.
      Unlocatable. Cited in O'Daniel (1971.B16).

1940 A BOOKS

1   PIQUION, RENÉ. Langston Hughes: Un Chant Nouveau. Port au
Prince, Haiti: Imprimérie de l'État, 159 pp.
      No page of contents divides this work into chapters.
Hughes was a cosmopolitan of the world and a writer
universally known. He perceives the plight of all
races but expresses the spiritual depths of his own. One
technique concerns his capturing of the rhythms rooted in

the African jungles. His emotion and power of imagination also excel. By being completely social, his verses are realistic.

1940 B SHORTER WRITINGS

1   ARVEY, VERNA. "Langston Hughes: Crusader," Opportunity, 18 (December 18), 363-364.
    Hughes has the gift of laughter--at himself, others, and most events. Since he gives poems to Black editors and forgets that someone else might have paid more money, Hughes's most popular quality is generosity. He crusades for the Negro race as a whole.

2   BONTEMPS, ARNA. "Introduction," to Langston Hughes: Un Chant Nouveau, by René Piquion. Port au Prince, Haiti: Imprimérie de l'État, pp. i-xvi.
    Hughes's Haitian journey made a lasting impression on him. He was a great lover of simple people.

3   LEWIS, THEOPHILUS. "Adventurous Life," Crisis, 47 (December), 395-396.
    Hughes is sufficiently important in Negro literature, perhaps in American, to deserve a biography. He may be too young, however. He mentions no really great men or women of the time. His narrative, rather, "refers to only the near-great, the shabby and the picturesque." Hughes expressed the major tone of his generation, a mingling of souciance with revolt. Because his poetry is dated, his prose may last longer. The Weary Blues may pass but Not Without Laughter will endure. The Ways of White Folks will also last. Many of its stories are among the finest that this reviewer has seen in American fiction. The Big Sea adds to his volume of prose. Enthusiasm and candor assure that the work will survive.

4   RUGOFF, MILTON. "Negro Writer's Heap of Living," NYHTB (Sunday, August 25), p. 5.
    The Big Sea is not bitter because Hughes is not. Rambling and anecdotal, the book has a friendly tone. Its tolerance, simplicity, and unpretentiousness border on the naive.

5   VILLARD, OSWALD GARRISON. "The Negro Intellectual," SatR, 22 (August 31), 12.
    On The Big Sea. Hughes's "absolute intellectual honesty and frankness" moved me. Looking at white and Negro worlds with rare objectivity, the writer "paints it exactly as he

1940

sees it." The Big Sea lacks any trace of self-pity. This
moving and worthwhile book should have been written. It
is a "most valuable contribution to the struggle of the
Negro for life and justice and freedom in America."

6   WOODS, CATHERINE. "A Negro Intellectual Tells His Life Story."
     NYTBR (August 25), p. 5.
         Hughes's autobiography manifests an unusual spirit and
     a significant time. Its lasting worth lies in its sensi-
     tivity, poise, candidness, reticence, realism, and lack
     of bitterness.

7   WRIGHT, RICHARD. "Forerunner and Ambassador," NR, 103
     (July-December), 600-601.
         Hughes freed Negro literature from timidity as Theodore
     Dreiser freed American literature from puritanism. As an
     ambassador of the race, Hughes represented its plight in
     the "court of world opinion." Since his travels freed him
     from middle class opinions, Hughes has a range of interest
     that no other Negro in his time possesses. He writes of
     the Negro Renaissance with "humor, urbanity, and
     objectivity."

1941 A BOOKS - NONE

1941 B SHORTER WRITINGS

1   BROWN, STERLING and ARTHUR P. DAVIS. The Negro Caravan. New
     York: Dryden Press, passim.
         The Way of White Folks is unusual because a Negro author
     uses satire to reveal the attitudes of whites toward Ne-
     groes. In short stories such as "Professor," Hughes's
     satire is directed at Negroes themselves. This writer is
     the most versatile of the New Negroes and the most eminent.
     His life has been a modern odyssey. He has met all kinds
     of people in all corners of the world, including Africa,
     Asia, Europe, and America.

2   CARGILL, OSCAR. Intellectual America: Ideas on the March.
     New York: MacMillan, p. 511.
         Earnest treatment of an insoluble problem makes Nigger
     Heaven take a place with Langston Hughes's Not Without
     Laughter and Miss Stein's "Melantcha" as one of the best
     fictional treatments of the Negro in American letters. The
     book, incidentally, is enhanced by the songs and snatches
     of Blues contributed by Langston Hughes.

18

3   EMBREE, EDWIN R. "A Poet's Story," SG, 30 (March), 96.
        Although The Big Sea is no great epic, it is a grand
     tale and an adventure story. Despite its being a story of
     a colored America, one finds "little searching of soul on
     questions of caste and class." The story is of a poet but
     not of a highbrow. It is written in beautiful English.

4   FORD, NICK AARON. "I Teach Negro Literature," CE, 2 (March),
     530-541.
        Hughes is the "most original of the Negro poets." He
     has shown his genius by numerous gems. No other poet in
     American literature has imagery more meaningful and touch-
     ing than that in "The Negro Speaks of Rivers."

5   HEROD, HENRIETTA L. "The Big Sea," Phylon, 2 (Spring), 94-96.
        Although often amusing, vivid, and sincere, The Big Sea
     is not a great book. In spots the work has problems of
     content and style, but it is never propaganda.

1942 A BOOKS - NONE

1942 B SHORTER WRITINGS

1   ANON. Review of Shakespeare in Harlem, The Nation, 155
     (August 8), 119.
        Being Afro-American, Shakespeare in Harlem is in the
     blues mood. Since it attempts a folkloric atmosphere, the
     break is lugubrious. The lyrics are sincere and readable.
     This is contemporary verse that is tragic and light.

2   COLUMN, MARY M. "The New Books of Poetry," NYTBR (March 22),
     p. 9.
        On Shakespeare in Harlem. Hughes has strong emotions,
     uses the form and vocabulary of the blues and spirituals.
     His imagination and intelligence, however, do not rival
     these. Although expressing only one type of Negro, the
     Harlemite, the book gives an "insight into the African
     mind." The Negro of Shakespeare in Harlem, is "immensely
     sad, even hopeless." "Death in Harlem," the second sec-
     tion, contains the most impressive poems.

3   DODSON, OWEN. "Shakespeare in Harlem," Phylon, 11 (Fall),
     337-338.
        Although being superior in format, Shakespeare in Harlem
     is a "careless surface job" that is unworthy of Hughes. He
     is "backing into the future looking at the past."

1942

4   HAYS, H. R. "To Be Sung or Shouted," Poetry, 60 (April-
    September), 223-224.
        On Shakespeare in Harlem. This book of light verse has
    charm and spontaneity. Without much concern for formal
    pattern, Hughes writes easily. His folk poems are perhaps
    the best.

5   KREYMBORG, ALFRED. "Seven American Poets," SatR, 25 (April), 9.
        On Shakespeare in Harlem. McKnight Kauffer's drawings
    are delightful. The verses remind one of such mastersingers
    of vaudeville as Bert Williams and Eddie Leonard. The poems
    reveal a subtle blending of tragedy and comedy, which is a
    rare, difficult, and exquisite art.

6   WALTON, EDNA LOU. "Nothing New Under the Sun," NM, 43
    (June), 23.
        Hughes only writes as he always has. His poems, close
    to folk songs, indicate no awareness of the changed war
    world. They are not profoundly class or race conscious.
    Easily listened to, they do not invoke sufficient thought.

1944 A BOOKS - NONE

1944 B SHORTER WRITINGS

1   EMBREE, EDWIN R. "Langston Hughes," in 13 Against the Odds.
    New York: Viking Press, pp. 129-30.
        Hughes is one of the country's most prolific writers of
    blues. Critics and reviewers hailed his work, but Negroes
    viciously attacked it. Although he has always been a left-
    ist in his political thinking, no "church" claimed his
    spirit, not even that of the Party. Many friends love him,
    and he is one of few men who are equally popular with
    whites and coloreds. Being boyish in his eagerness, he
    is natural in his manners: "He is as modest a man as ever
    lived, free of arrogance or prejudice, balanced with a keen
    and subtle sense of humor."

2   O'SHEEL, THOMAS YOSELOFF. "Introduction," in Seven Poets in
    Search of an Answer. New York: Bernard Ackerman, pp. 1-4.
        Hughes deserves equal praise for his universality and
    for his dedication to his own people. To simple rhyme, he
    sets moving passion. "He will not let America forget the
    shame of lynch law and Jim Crow."

1945 A BOOKS - NONE

1945 B SHORTER WRITINGS

1   ANON. "Birth of a Poet," <u>MJ</u>, 36 (February 5), 12-16.
At 43 Hughes is the "outstanding poet in America." He
has been to Hollywood once, and his chief work there was
writing lyrics. He has found the greatest prejudice not
among editors but in the area of jobs when Negroes want
to compete for salaried positions in writing. Condensed
1945.B2.

2   ANON. "Birth of a Poet," <u>ND</u>, 36 (April), 41-42.
Condensed version of 1945.B1.

1946 A BOOKS - NONE

1946 B SHORTER WRITINGS

1   KAMP, STELLA. "Langston Hughes Speaks to Young Writers,"
<u>Opportunity</u>, 24 (April), 73.
Hughes advises young writers: "Give your work away"
[at first].

1947 A BOOKS - NONE

1947 B SHORTER WRITINGS

*1 BABB, INEZ JOHNSON. "Bibliography of Langston Hughes, Negro
Poet." Unpublished Masters Thesis, Pratt Institute Library
School.
Unlocatable. Cited in Loff (Brooks: 1973.B6).

2   CREEKMORE, HUBERT. "Poems by Langston Hughes," <u>NYTBR</u> (May 4),
p. 10.
On <u>Fields of Wonder</u>. Beauty and leanness of lyrics distinguish the volume. Racial identity or regionalism seldom
inspire the work which is strained and lacking. An easier
power came in the earlier verses. Here despite a variety
of subject matter, the collection is monotonous. Nevertheless, Hughes's poems "have lyricism and honesty of
vision."

3   LECHLINTER, RUTH. "Stevens, Cullen, Hughes, Greenberg,"
<u>NYHTBR</u> (August 31), p. 4
In contrast to Countee Cullen's formality, Hughes's work
has always been simple and colloquial, or has had a folk
charm. Some of the nature pieces remind one of Sandburg

1947

or of the artless and childlike quality found in Vachel
Lindsay. The theme is too narrow, the patterns too similar, to make an effective book.

4   WOODRUFF, BERTRAM L.   "Of Myth and Symbol," Phylon, 8
        (Summer), 198-200.
            Fields of Wonder "charms with its simplicity." For the
        reader, Hughes uses personal symbols to awaken "old memo-
        ries and reflections." Like Countee Cullen, Hughes is
        deeply religious.

1948 A BOOKS - NONE

1948 B SHORTER WRITINGS

1   BARTON, REBECCA CHALMER.   "The Big Sea: Langston Hughes,"
        Witnesses for Freedom. New York: Harper and Brothers,
        passim.
            Perhaps the measure of his talent lies in the aptness
        with which he could be called poet-sociologist. His
        naiveté is disarming. His leaving Columbia was probably
        an unconscious rejection of his father's worship of success.
        Open-mindedness and the lack of egotism enable him to
        profit most from the Harlem Renaissance, which he has
        reconstructed intimately and faithfully. He met or knew
        all of the following: Rebecca West, Somerset Maugham,
        Carl Van Vechten, Alfred Knopf, Louis Untermeyer, Waldo
        Frank, Hugh Walpole, Jascha Heifetz, Salvador Dali, and
        Rudolph Valentino. Hughes disrespects institutions or con-
        ventions that "kill the spirit of truth." Although he
        looks for the good in all individuals, he reserves a
        special loyalty for the Negro race to which he was born.

2   GLOSTER, HUGH M.   Negro Voices in American Fiction.   Chapel
        Hill: University of North Carolina Press, pp. 219-222.
            After the publication of Not Without Laughter in 1930,
        Hughes aligned himself to the proletarian school of writers.
        "Father to Son," in The Ways of White Folks, is only one of
        fourteen stories that aggressively voice proletarian ideol-
        ogy. The Ways of White Folks is "the outstanding indict-
        ment of Nordicism in modern American fiction." Reprint
        of 1965.B3.

3   TOLSON, M. B.   "Books and Authors: Let My People Go," SJ, 4
        (Fall-Winter), 41-43.
            Fittingly illustrated by Jacob Lawrence, One Way Ticket
        reveals that Hughes has not lost the touch of The Weary

Blues. Few American poets have equalled him in faithful-
ness to his milieu and its artistic expression. Hughes
portrays the urban Negro, as Paul Lawrence Dunbar did the
rural Negro. Having transformed naive ballads into conscious art, he is the "blues troubador par excellence."
His sensitive ear catches the nuances of comedy and tragedy.
Despite differences of technique, Hughes's "Florida Road
Workers," reminds one of Archibald MacLeish's "Burying
Ground by the Ties" in Frescoes for Mr. Rockefeller's City.

1949 A BOOKS - NONE

1949 B SHORTER WRITINGS

1   CHANDLER, G. LEWIS. "Selfsameness and a Promise," Phylon, 10
     (Summer), 189-191.
         One Way Ticket has all the traits that distinguish
     Hughes's works: humor, irony, tragedy, folksiness, earth-
     iness, subtlety, puckishness, and hope. One notices the
     universal "I" that is reminiscent of Whitman. Hughes is a
     synecdochist, for he uses the racial as a means to achieve
     the universal.

2   DAICHES, DAVID. "Poetry of Negro Moods," NYHTBR (January 9),
     p. 4.
         On One Way Ticket. As a documentary of the Negro, this
     is "worlds apart" from the "subtle distillation" of meaning
     aimed at by other serious contemporary poets. Jazz and
     folk rhythm combine to create a "strange and soul sense of
     inevitability."

3   HUMPHRIES, ROLPHE. "Verse Chronical," The Nation, 168
     (January 15), 80.
         On One Way Ticket. Hughes's poetry has the virtue of
     forbearance, a theme which he treats with great restraint:
     basic vocabulary, simple rhymes, short line, no violence,
     no hyperbole. Hughes should try to be more elaborate, in-
     volved, and complex. He should be less the spokesman and
     more the individual; he should exploit more fully his edu-
     cation, travel, reading, and music other than the blues.

4   PARKER, JOHN W. "Tomorrow in the Writings of Langston Hughes,"
     CE, 10 (May), 438-441.
         Carl Van Vechten called Hughes the "Negro Poet Laureate."
     The latter possibly became the "most representative expo-
     nent of the new spirit in Negro literature." Hughes makes
     clear a self-conscious revolt against the American scheme.

1949

> If night or darkness offers him a challenge, it never offers
> him disillusionment. He has mainly followed the course of
> a social poet.

5   WEBSTER, HARVEY CURTIS. "One-Way Poetry," Poetry, 75
     (October 1949-March 1950), 300-302.
          Hughes's poetry has been neglected because it is "so far
     removed" from the formal traditions that the dominant school
     of criticism respects. Having limited subject matter, he
     tends to write the same poem many times. Hughes writes
     about the "surface of things" and the levels of emotion
     that concern the individual of a group rather than one
     human being. He "never moves one deeply."

1950 A BOOKS - NONE

1950 B SHORTER WRITINGS

1   ALLEN, WILLIAM. "The Barrier: A Critique," Phylon, 11
     (2nd Quarter), 134-136.
          In The Barrier, John Meyerowitz rewords Mulatto into an
     opera. Hughes believes that the opera should develop in
     America and that he should write the libretto for this.

2   PFAFF, WILLIAM. Review of Simple Speaks His Mind, Commonweal,
     52 (May 26), 239.
          Although the effect is polemical more than artistic,
     it is painless. It is a "strong and sometimes bitter de-
     fense of the Harlem Negro." The tone is humorous but sen-
     sitive and dignified. The social impact hits the white
     reader. The work is "neither art nor truth" but approaches
     being both.

3   REDDING, J. SAUNDERS. "What it Means to be Colored," NYHTBR
     (June), p. 13.
          As a tradition, Simple goes back to the horse-sense
     humorists of the 1880's and 90's. He has familial ties to
     Charles Hebner Clark's "Cooley," the creations of Josh
     Billings and Artemus Ward, and the "Mr. Dooley" of Finley
     Peter Dunne. Hughes has "completely fulfilled the tradi-
     tion and perhaps gone a step beyond." Clark's Cooley and
     Dunne's Dooley show the contemporary mind at work on
     current problems, but Hughes's Simple "ranges the universe."

4   SMITH, WILLIAM GARDNER. "Simple's Dialogues," NR, 123
     (September), 20.

Simple is the "voice of the American Negro as few have
heard him speak." The book will be a revelation for those
who without pretension want to know the thoughts of the
"ordinary Negro."

5 SMYTHE, HUGH M. "Hughesesque Insight," Crisis, 57 (June),
377-378.
On Simple Speaks His Mind. The volume provides "entertainment unmatched in literature of recent times." This
is one of Hughes's finest contributions. Combining humor
and sociology, it is a tour de force that all can enjoy.

6 THOMPSON, EVA BELL. "Belles Lettres," ND, 8-9 (July), 40-41.
Hughes is the "writingest colored man in the world." He
writes strictly at night and burns the bulb until 4 a.m.
For breakfast he eats anything from Post Toasties to pot-
licker. He is a connoisseur of foods worldwide, but is
happy with okra, gumbo, red beans, and rice.

7 VAN VECHTEN, CARL. "Dialogues But Barbed," NYTBR (May 7),
p. 10.
On Simple Speaks His Mind. Completely frank in his
opinions about whites, Simple "dislikes them intensely."
Although the problem of race is never absent, the "flow of
the book is light-hearted and easy." Only a Negro as wise
as Langston Hughes could have written the book.

1951 A BOOKS - NONE

1951 B SHORTER WRITINGS

1 CHANDLER, G. LEWIS. "For Your Recreation and Reflection,"
Phylon, 12 (Spring), 94-95.
Simple Speaks His Mind demonstrates once again Hughes's
style. This mixes common life, genial humor, and uncomfortable satire. This work is another Shakespeare in Harlem,
One Way Ticket, or Sweet Flypaper of Life done in a series
of prose vignettes.

2 DEUTSCH, BABETTE. "Waste Land of Harlem," NYTBR (May 6),
p. 23.
On Montage of a Dream Deferred. The verses invite
approval but lapse into a sentimentality that stifles real
feeling. As a whole, the book "leaves one less responsive
to the poet's achievement than conscious of the limitations
of folk art." Hughes should be more rigorous in the use of
his undeniable gifts and more like his French contemporaries.

1951

3   HUMPHRIES, ROLFE. "Verse Chronicle," <u>The Nation</u>, 72
     (March 17), 256.
       <u>Montage of a Dream Deferred</u> confuses me, as work by
     Hughes often does. Since a split exists between Hughes the
     individual and Hughes the spokesman, the statement here is
     both "oversimplified and theatrical."

*4   O'DANIEL, THERMAN B. "A Langston Hughes Bibliography," <u>CLA
     Bulletin</u>, 7 (Spring), 12-13.
       Unlocatable, but twice revised and expanded: 1968.B22;
     1971.B16.

5   PARKER, JOHN W. "Poetry of Harlem in Transition," <u>Phylon</u>, 12
     (Summer), 195-197.
       In <u>Montage of a Dream Deferred</u> Hughes has "rejuvenated
     the Harlem theme of the mid-twenties, and re-asserted his
     faith in popular verse, particularly that which draws upon
     popular Negro folk music." This is his first book-length
     poem.

6   REDDING, SAUNDERS. "Langston Hughes in an Old Vein with New
     Rhythms," <u>NYHTBR</u> (March 11), p. 5.
       Hughes proves himself again the "provocative folk singer,"
     and has returned to the spiritual heritage of the Negro
     Renaissance. Although the images probe into old emotions
     and experiences, they show nothing new. His idiom is
     constant, but now he adapts it to be-bop rather than to
     jazz. Hughes has always required a sophisticated ear, but
     he is too concerned with sustaining his "reputation as an
     experimenter."

1952 A BOOKS - NONE

1952 B SHORTER WRITINGS

1   ANON. Review of <u>Poemas</u>, <u>Crisis</u>, 59 (November), 606.
       Often Hughes's colloquialisms sound strange in
     Castillian because the basic structure of Spanish is still
     Latin. These minor shortcomings detract from the value of
     the book. He has a wide audience in Latin America, where
     his verses have been anthologized and translated. Hughes
     is less a "race poet" than a proletarian writer. For the
     inarticulate masses, he voices suffering and aspiration.

2   BETSCHEL, L. S. "Thinking Toward a Better World," <u>NYHTBR</u>
     (November 16), p. 32.

1952

To both Negro and white children, The First Book of
Negroes will be illuminating. It will "give young Negroes
pride in their heritage and in their American citizenship."

3   BONTEMPS, ARNA. "Black & Bubbling," SatR, 35 (April 5), 17.
On Laughing to Keep from Crying. More than many people,
Hughes has enjoyed being Negro. The depression of the
thirties shadows all the stories and provides continuity.
Hughes's literary art depends on intuition and mother-wit.
His work is for those who judge with the heart as well as
with the head.

4   COOPERMAN, STANLEY. "Fiction Before Problem," NR, 126
(May 5), 21.
Laughing to Keep from Crying gives more insight into
racism than even the ablest "problem fiction" can achieve.
The writing is lean and compact.

5   DAVIS, ARTHUR P. "The Harlem of Langston Hughes's Poetry,"
Phylon, 13 (4th Quarter), 276-283.
Hughes has written about Harlem more often and completely
than any other poet. His characters vainly search to make
Harlem a part of the American Dream. With Hughes, Harlem
is both place and symbol. By portraying one black ghetto,
he describes all black ghettos in America. Reprint 1966.B1.

6   HEDDEN, WORTH TUTTLE. "Laughter and Tears across the Barriers
of Race," NYHTBR (Sunday, March 30), p. 32.
On Laughing to Keep from Crying. Hughes's advantage
over white American authors is that he does not look down
on the country from the grandstand of the majority but
mingles with individuals on all levels.

7   LLOYD, HORTENSE D. Review of Tambourines to Glory, NER, 10,
100-101.
The story is panoramic, compellingly told, compact, and
lucid.

8   MEIER, AUGUST. "Poignancy," Crisis, 59 (June-July), 398-399.
On Laughing to Keep from Crying. Two of the best stories
are "One Friday Morning" and "Professor." The short fiction
as a whole is told with insight and good humor. The volume
is entertaining, pungent, and first-rate.

9   MOON, BUCKLIN. "Laughter, Tears, and the Blues," NYTBR
(March 23), p. 4.
On Laughing to Keep from Crying. More important writers
than Hughes may have lived, and they may have worked a

1952

broader canvas, but few have been so "versatile or workman-
like." Although these are not the best of Hughes's short
stories, they are very good. Since racial thinking has
changed, some are archaic. Nevertheless, many writers have
said less in an overblown novel than is said here in twelve
pages.

10 PARKER, JOHN W. "Literature of the Negro Ghetto," Phylon, 13
(Fall), 257-258.
On Laughing to Keep from Crying. Spontaneity and charm
all but assure the reader's interest. Hughes's creative
genius consists in blending a humor of characterization
with a humor of situation. The unwavering pessimism leaves
one wondering if Hughes remembers his faith in our tomor-
rows. Laughing to Keep from Crying pleads eloquently for
social awareness and justice nationally and worldwide.

1953 A BOOKS - NONE

1953 B SHORTER WRITINGS

1 ANON. Review of Simple Takes a Wife, Crisis, 60 (October),
506.
As in the previous volume, Simple speaks his mind. Now,
however, the conversation concerns women, marriage, and
Harlem rooming houses. The atmosphere and idiom are
Harlem, and the punning sometimes annoys.

2 BERRY, ABNER. "Not So Simple," MaM, 6 (September), 55-58.
On Simple Takes a Wife. In the term "Be-bop," Simple
uses the Negro folk characteristic and treats a serious
problem, police brutality, with humorous derision. Hughes
has the perfect protagonist of race. Simple Speaks His
Mind had a wider range of topics. Simple has toned down
since Hughes has been the "guest" of Senator Joseph McCarthy.
In the real inquest, Hughes fared less well than Simple
did in the fictional world. In the future, Hughes should
portray Simple in a work situation. Although Hughes displays a reporter's eye and a novelist's ear, he fails to
give a realistic portrait of other people in the ghetto.
By portraying the richness of Negro life, Hughes's work
sharply opposes the "arty" degeneracy of writers like
Richard Wright and Ralph Ellison. Simple fails to prophesy
the future but delightfully portrays the present.

3 BONTEMPS, ARNA. "That Not So Simple Sage, Mr. Simple,"
NYHTBR (June 14).

28

The Simple books fit no convenient category. Simple Takes a Wife is neither a novel nor a collection of short stories. This volume has a bite. To call it humor does not suffice.

4   BROOKS, HALLIE BEACHEM. "For Young Readers," Phylon, 14 (Fall), 343-344.
On First Book of Negroes. Since the lack of organization is a serious weakness, Hughes might have helped his young readers by finding more appropriate groupings. Nevertheless, many stories are told in an inspiring and dramatic manner--especially those of Estaven, Toussaint, Christophe, and Harriet Tubman. Although Ursula Koering's illustrations are "attractive, vivid, and realistic," the drawings of real-life personalities lack true resemblance.

5   McBROWN, GERTRUDE PARTHENIA. "First Book of Negroes," NHB, 16 (Fall), 94-95.
Hughes has produced a work of rare genius. He has combined the teller's art, the poet's insight, and the researcher's accuracy.

6   SHAGALOFF, JUNE. "First Book of Negroes," Crisis, 60 (January), 62-63.
Hughes's presentation brings about pride and admiration. He succeeds in the attempt to mock subtly the stereotypes of Negroes and to counteract such stereotypes. He integrates Negro life with that of Americans of other races and nationalities.

1954 A BOOKS - NONE

1954 B SHORTER WRITINGS

1   ANON. "The Anisfield-Wolf Awards," SatR, 37 (April), 20.
Simple Takes a Wife wins the prize for a book or group of books that best illuminate racial problems. Serious understanding underlies the humor of the volume. In its warm and personal expression, the reader finds the "striving and frustration of the urban Negro trying to take his place in a white world."

2   B., E. L. "Seventeen Leaders," NYTBR (May 2), p. 26.
On Famous American Negroes. The sketches of lesser-known men make this a valuable contribution to the biography shelf.

1954

3   DAVIS, ARTHUR P.   "Jesse B. Semple: Negro American," <u>Phylon</u>,
    15, 21-28.
        Semple's most appealing trait is that he is a comic
    figure at which Negroes can laugh and not be ashamed.
    Semple represents the thinking of the average Negro.

1955 A BOOKS - NONE

1955 B SHORTER WRITINGS

1   B., A.   Review of <u>The First Book of Jazz</u>, <u>SatR</u>, 38 (January-
    June), 55.
        Clearly and precisely, <u>The First Book of Jazz</u> defines
    jazz and traces its origin. This book will begin the edu-
    cation of any novice.

2   BALL, JOHN.   "Hughes on Jazz," <u>MidJ</u>, 7-8 (Summer), 195-196.
        It is amazing that Hughes can do so much in a short
    book. This primer is rarely controversial, most readable,
    and interesting. He should have mentioned the George Lewis
    ragtime band. The citations of blues records should be
    clearer and should refer to obtainable editions. These
    citations are "inadequate to give a good understanding of
    archaic and classic blues." The faults are few; the good
    points many.

3   BELSCHEL, LOUISE S.   "For Boys and Girls," <u>NYHTBR</u> (February 27),
    p. 10.
        On <u>The First Book of Jazz</u>. Hughes selects and simpli-
    fies but does not "write down."

4   DAVIS, ARTHUR P.   "The Tragic Mulatto Theme in Six Works of
    Langston Hughes," <u>Phylon</u>, 16 (4th Quarter), 195-204.
        The verse "Cross" in <u>The Weary Blues</u> is the original
    statement of the theme in Hughes's work. The writer uses
    yellow as a symbol for the degradation and unhappiness that
    supposedly result from situations of mixed racial blood.

5   FELD, ROSE.   "The Warm Human Essence of Harlem," <u>NYHTBR</u>
    (December 13), p. 31.
        On <u>Sweet Flypaper of Life</u>. This lyric narrative probably
    has fewer than a thousand words, but it glowingly portrays
    human experience.

6   H., V.   "Langston Hughes: The First Book of Jazz," <u>Hor</u>, 31
    (June), 175.

1956

The book will appeal to the older child, especially one who has been interested in jazz or has been a record collector.

7   HATCH, ROBERT R. Review of Sweet Flypaper of Life, The Nation, 181 (December), 538.
    Its pictures make this a work of quality. The story is perceptive and tender, but also cute and patronizing.

8   MILLSTEIN, GILBERT. "While Sister Mary Sticks Around," NYTBR (November 27), p. 5.
    On Sweet Flypaper of Life. This document is delicate and lovely. Its verisimilitude is astonishing; its tone is quiet and lively. The rhythms are soft and emphatic; the insights, constant. The story and pictures justify each other.

9   PARKER, JOHN W. "American Jazz: Composite of Many Influences," Phylon (Fall), pp. 318-319.
    First Book of Jazz underscores two tendencies: Hughes's shift from poetry to prose and his change to juvenile litera-ture. Hughes lists the who's who of jazz artists--most notably, Louis Armstrong. First Book of Jazz is the first history of jazz that a Negro has written.

10 SMYTHE, MARCEL M. Review of Famous American Negroes, Crisis, 62 (Spring), 58.
    This book is for the young. Hughes has created readable and human biographies that transform the shadowy figures of history books into flesh and blood people.

1956 A BOOKS - NONE

1956 B SHORTER WRITINGS

1   IVY, JAMES. Review of Pictorial History of the Negro in America, Crisis, 64 (February), 132.
    One should congratulate the authors for promoting the Negro's history through pictorial representation. More pages should be devoted to the last twenty years. The last section, "Toward One World," shows a paucity of pictures.

2   OTTLEY, ROI. "Politics, Poetry, and Peccadillos," SatR, 39 (November 17), 35.
    Hughes is perhaps the "most versatile and best known Negro poet in the world." In I Wonder as I Wander he has written warmly about the people whom he encountered in his

31

1956

travels around the globe. I liked Emma, Moscow's Mammy
and expatriate from Dixie, best. In a personal history,
interwoven with personal narratives, the book is a "sort
of vagabondia with a dash of racialism."

3   PARKER, JOHN W. "The Bright, Right Side," CC, 73 (August 1),
     905.
          On Sweet Flypaper of Life. For nearly thirty years,
     Hughes has been concerned with Harlem as a place and symbol.
     This volume distinguishes itself by showing the "sunshine
     etching the shadow." There is humor of characterization and
     situation. The Negro woman has taken a "sound lashing" in
     many of Hughes's books, but here she is maternal and married.

4   _____. "Parcels of Humanity," Crisis, 63 (February), 124-125.
          This makes similar points about Sweet Flypaper of Life
     (see 1956.B3). Love and family life are the focus in the
     Black community. The Negro woman is portrayed more favor-
     ably as being clean, loyal, and motherly.

5   REDDING, SAUNDERS. "The American Negro's Role in History,"
     NYHTBR (November 18), p. 7.
          Fortunately, Hughes and Meltzer have avoided the academic
     historian's restraint and achieved a historic sweep.

6   _____. "Travels of Langston Hughes's Events as Seen in Pass-
     ing," NYHTBR (December 23), p. 6.
          I Wonder as I Wander is "frank and charming," although
     one sees neither events nor people in depth. Hughes wan-
     dered more than wondered.

1957 A BOOKS - NONE

1957 B SHORTER WRITINGS

1   APTHEKER, HERBERT. "Negro Panorama," Mainstream, 10
     (February), 62-63.
          On Pictorial History of the Negro in America. On the
     whole, Hughes and Meltzer "realized their vision well and
     produced an excellent gift-volume of permanent value."
     The scarce illustrations are greatly interesting; the
     quality of reproduction is very high, the tone anti-racist
     or "New Dealish." Being descriptive rather than analytical,
     the work strives for simplicity but occasionally "falls
     into simplification." Factual errors occur, but not in
     abundance, and they are not very serious. The message
     is to eliminate Jim Crow, and the pictures make the work
     enjoyable.

2   FORD, NICK AARON. "Odyssey of a Literary Man," Phylon, 18
     (Spring), 88-89.
         On I Wonder as I Wander. Hughes has a fourfold task:
     to entertain; to present historical and cultural informa-
     tion about far-away places; to point out attitudes of race
     and color in the various parts of the world; and to reveal
     his philosophy of art and life. Sometimes the second
     attempt becomes extraneous, although legend and anecdote
     most often serve the purpose well. Impatient with dis-
     crimination and segregation, Hughes is seldom bitter. The
     work has several shortcomings. It comes too late and
     overemphasizes amatory experiences. Constantly referring
     to critical praise of Hughes's work, it suggests immaturity.
     One finds too much attention to gossip and hearsay. Never-
     theless, the volume will profit and please those who have
     time to read it.

3   GEHMAN, RICHARD. "Fee, Free, Enterprise," SatR, 41
     (November 22), 19-20.
         On Tambourines to Glory. The cleanness and simplicity
     of this volume remind one of the gospel songs of Clara
     Ward. Hughes draws characters in "bold, Rouault-like
     strokes." One should read this funny book aloud. It
     reaffirms Hughes's talent and his "belief in the miracle
     of human behavior."

4   JACKSON, LUTHER. Review of I Wonder as I Wander, Crisis, 64
     (February), 119-120.
         Hughes is the last practicing writer of that group that
     came to influence during the 1920's. Like most of his
     works, this one lacks the reasoning that would explain race
     relations. Hughes never tells on himself or his friends--
     two autobiographies notwithstanding. His stance on the
     USSR is middle of the road. The best sections of the book
     are the first two, which deal with hungry nights in the
     Caribbean and lecture tours of southern Negro colleges.
     His account of his trip from Daytona Beach, Florida, to
     New York with an artist friend and the late Mary Bethune is
     best.

5   _____. Review of Simple Stakes a Claim, Crisis, 64 (May),
     576-577.
         With Simple, Hughes has struck commercial gold. The
     Broadway production of Simply Heavenly shows clearly the
     author's awareness of racial sensitivities, but Simple
     Stakes a Claim is Grade A and pure. Simple reaches new
     heights of "racial indignation and disgust."

1957

6   MILLSTEIN, GILBERT. "Negro Everyman," <u>NYTBR</u> (September),
       p. 41.
             Like the earlier volumes, <u>Simple Stakes a Claim</u> is funny,
       sharp, indignant and tolerant--even of whites. It demon-
       strates the stupidities, callousness, and cruelties of
       whites and Negroes alike. All of the Simple books should
       be bound together in one volume.

7   PARKER, JOHN W. "The Remarkable Mr. Simple Again," <u>Phylon</u>,
       18 (Winter), 435-436.
             <u>Simple Stakes a Claim</u> defines a situation in which Brown
       Americans of a Northern ghetto face reality and assume that
       tomorrow will be better. <u>Simple Stakes a Claim</u> is a fresh
       and vital collection. The unity of action, concerning
       Simple, and the unity of impression hold the volume to-
       gether. As in <u>Simple Speaks His Mind</u>, <u>Simple Takes a Wife</u>,
       and <u>Sweet Flypaper of Life</u>, Hughes uses humor as an approach
       to the problems of race. Now Simple is as American as
       "turkey at Thanksgiving." <u>Simple Stakes a Claim</u> will add
       to Hughes's stature.

8   _____. "Negro Folklore: Segment of American Culture," <u>CLAJ</u>,
       1-2 (November-March), 185-186.
             For these men, the plight of the American Negro has
       become an obsession.

*9   _____. "Simple: Symbol of a New Day," <u>CLAJ</u>, 1, No. 1.
             On <u>Simple Stakes a Claim</u>. Unlocatable. Listed in
       O'Daniel (1971.B16).

1958 A BOOKS - NONE

1958 B SHORTER WRITINGS

1   BONE, ROBERT. <u>Negro Novel in America</u>. New Haven: Yale
       University Press, pp. 75-77.
             Laughter is the central symbol of <u>Not Without Laughter</u>.
       The problem with the novel is that Hughes tries to reject
       the Protestant ethic (joy is wrong) while retaining the
       success drive on which it is based. The novel might better
       be written around Harriet who emerges from a life of pros-
       titution to become "Princess of the Blues." Hughes was
       unprepared to meet the rigorous requirements of his form.
       The work is ideologically confused and structurally defec-
       tive. It gives a final impression of "sprawling formless-
       ness." Hughes's importance, however, far transcends that
       of <u>Not Without Laughter</u>.

2   BONOSKY, PHILLIP. "Humor and Hope," Mainstream, 11
       (January), 53-56.
          On Simple Stakes a Claim. Simple is a contemporary
       Mr. Dooley. The interlocutor's conventional language
       "contrasts deliciously with Simple's tasty idioms."

3   BONTEMPS, ARNA. "How the Money Rolled In," NYHT (December 17),
       p. 4.
          On Tambourines to Glory. The story is ribald and effort-
       less. On the surface, it is as artless as a folk ballad.
       The tone is fond and humorous. Hughes's writings become
       even more an "affair of the heart with Harlem." Although
       hilarious, Tambourines to Glory is no joke.

*4 HENTOFF, NAT. "Langston Hughes: He Found Poetry in the Blues,"
       Mayfair (August), pp. 26-27.
          Unlocatable. Listed in O'Daniel (1971.A2).

5   JAHN, JANHEINZ. Muntu: The New African Culture. Germany:
       Eugene Diedrichs Dusseldorf, pp. 200-204.
          In Hughes's verses we find continuously the notes of
       African ancestry. For English version, see 1961.B5. See
       also 1968.B15.

6   MILLSTEIN, GILBERT. "Laura and Essie Belle," NYTBR
       (November 23), p. 51.
          On Tambourines to Glory. "The novel is a sort of Negro
       Elmer Gantry." It is skillful and engaging, but minor in
       light of Hughes's other productions. Here the same irony
       and humor which distinguish the Simple tales fog the
       thesis.

1959 A BOOKS - NONE

1959 B SHORTER WRITINGS

1   BALDWIN, JAMES. "Sermons and Blues," NYTBR (March 29), p. 6.
          I am dismayed that Hughes has done so little with his
       genuine gifts. A more disciplined poet would have thrown
       much of this into the wastebasket (especially most of the
       last section). Hughes is at his best in brief sardonic
       asides or in lyrics like "Mother to Son" and "The Negro
       Speaks of Rivers." He has not forced the Blues into art
       "where their meaning would become clear and overwhelming."
       He is another American Negro who finds irreconcilable the
       war between his racial obligation and his responsibilities.

1959

2   BARDOLPH, RICHARD. "Part III, 1936-1959: Behold the Promised
    Land," The Negro Vanguard. New York: Holt, Rinehardt &
    Winston, pp. 203-243.
        In the 1930's, Hughes was already what he remains today:
    "the unofficial laureate of the race, personally young,
    ebullient, and amused."

3   CARDONA-HINE, ALVARO. "Open Handshake," Mainstream, 12
    (July), 55-56.
        Selected Poems of Langston Hughes results in a "limpid
    congregation of effortless rhyme and folk-like simplicity."
    Hughes understands the roots of Negro faith. Unmarred by
    conventional morality, these pages have politics in poetry.
    McKnight Kauffer's drawings, reproduced from Shakespeare
    in Harlem, do not always "merit their company." The
    verses on freedom and equality fail because they never
    surpass abstraction. Hughes's writing is flute-like,
    sweet, clear, and delicate.

4   DREW, FRASER. "Langston Hughes and My Students," Trace, 32,
    22-24.
        One of Drew's students writes to Hughes for help in her
    study of him. In reply, she receives the following:
    friendly letter, promise of assistance, sheaf of reprints,
    articles about Hughes's work, bibliography and press re-
    leases, theater programs, and inscribed photograph.

5   IVY, JAMES W. Review of The Book of Negro Humor, Crisis, 66
    (March), 181-182.
        The collection is remarkable and comprehensive. It is
    a skillful piece of writing.

6   JACKSON, BLYDEN. "A Golden Mean for the Negro Novel," CLAJ,
    3, no. 2 (December), 81-87.
        Like Richard Wright's Native Son, Ann Petry's The Street,
    William Gardner Smith's Last of the Conquerors, Ralph
    Ellison's Invisible Man, and John Oliver Killens's Young-
    blood, Not Without Laughter contrasts with Fauset's work.
    This basic group of novels portrays the black middle class
    as developing from the black masses and not the other way
    around.

7   LONG, RICHARD. Review of Tambourines to Glory, CLAJ, 2
    (March), 192-193.
        Having simplicity of plot and character, the novel has
    charm, too. It is a fable. Ever present is Hughes's mas-
    tery of Negro idiom.

8   PARKER, JOHN W. "Another Revealing Facet of the Harlem Scene,"
      Phylon, 20 (Spring), 100-101.
            On Tambourines to Glory. In this urban folktale, one
      finds that the fusion of thirty-six segments is more mean-
      ingful than the parts. Organization stems from the consis-
      tency of mood and the unity of action. Handling of plot
      allows for suspense and movement. The work begins in medias
      res.

9   _____. "The Poetic Faith of a Social Poet," Phylon, (Summer)
      pp. 196-197.
            Selected Poems of Langston Hughes is vague in organiza-
      tion, since its eighteen chapters are "more formal than
      organic." The pieces are grouped by mood instead of by
      chronology or by type. To Hughes, poetry is "forever in
      the process of becoming." As a social writer, he believes
      that the chief purpose of poetry is to criticize life.

10 STAPLES, ELIZABETH. "Langston Hughes: Malevolent Force," AM,
      88 (January), 46-50.
            Hughes piles filth on filth, and his Negroes lack dig-
      nity and race pride. When extracted from Not Without
      Laughter, however, his short story "Guitar" provides a
      spontaneity of utterance and yields the heart of "primitive
      Negro artistry." Hughes has a long record of pro-Communism.

11 WATERHOUSE, KEITH. "New Novels," NS, 58 (July), 366.
            On Tambourines to Glory. The story is undemanding and
      Hughes quotes Negro hymns too often. In its "folksy way,"
      however, the novel is very amusing.

12 WINSLOW, HARRY F. Review of Selected Poems, Crisis, 66
      (October), 512-513.
            Here one finds the endurance and exuberance of spirit
      found only in the young. The verses should be dated so as
      to provide for some chronological approach. What would
      Hughes sound like if he treated the spiritual as well as
      the secular?

1960 A BOOKS - NONE

1960 B SHORTER WRITINGS

1   ANON. "Langston Hughes - 45th Spingarn Medalist," Crisis, 67
      (August-September), 422-423.
            Hughes becomes the first Spingarn medalist to receive
      the award directly from a member of the Spingarn family.

1960

The honor was presented at the closing session of the 51st annual NAACP convention in St. Paul on June 26 by Arthur B. Spingarn, who instituted the award in 1914. The latter praises Hughes as the first Negro in over a hundred years to support himself solely by his literary creations.

2   ISAACS, HAROLD. "Five Writers and Their African Ancestors," Phylon, 21 (3rd Quarter), 247-254.
Of all the literary figures in the 1920's, Hughes has proved himself the hardiest; of the poets who sang of Africa then, he alone had been there. To him laughter was a way of functioning, or coping with life. He achieved uniqueness as a poet by describing the life and people of the Negro ghetto. Their sights and sounds were his, as were their sorrow and sardonic humor.

1961 A BOOKS - NONE

1961 B SHORTER WRITINGS

1   BLESH, RUDI. "Jazz as a Marching Jubilee," NYHTB (Sunday, November 26), p. 4.
On Ask Your Mama: 12 Moods for Jazz. Not merely an observer of dark-skinned peoples, Hughes sings of the freedom that must belong to all or none. Ask Your Mama is a half-derisive and half-angry retort to people who exhibit bigotry, smugness, stupidity, selfishness, and blindness.

2   EMANUEL, JAMES. "Langston Hughes's First Short Story: Mary Winosky," Phylon, 22 (Fall), 267-272.
An English teacher at Central High in Cleveland, Ohio first saw the piece. Hughes had written it for a class assignment. The story both opens and closes in the spring-- in hope and the death of hope. The narrative style con- trasts with that of "Mother and Child" (1934) and finds new expression in more mature work: "Red Headed Baby," "On the Way Home," and "Home."

3   FITTS, DUDLEY. "A Trio of Singers," NYTBR (October 29), p. 16.
Review of Ask Your Mama. No canon of literary right or wrong can evaluate these pieces. Ask Your Mama recalls Vachel Lindsay's Congo. The voice is comparable to that of Cuban Nicholas Guillén or the Puerto Rican Luis Pales Matos; it is not, however, imitative. The development is parallel.

4   FORD, NICK AARON. "Battle of the Books: A Critical Survey of
     Significant Books By and About Negroes Published in 1960,"
     Phylon, 22 (Summer), pp. 126-127.
          Review of An African Treasury. The versatile and race-
     conscious Hughes deserves the thanks of all readers who are
     concerned about the "future of human freedom." Peter
     Abraham's "Episode in Malay Camp" is the most powerful and
     satisfying story.

5   JAHN, JANHEINZ. Muntu: The New African Culture. New York:
     Grove Press, pp. 200-204.
          Having a narrative "I" that shows social responsibility
     and using the image of the river, Hughes's verse "The Negro
     Speaks" is more African than is first apparent. One situ-
     ates Hughes between Thomas Mofolo, whose works show only
     African influence, and Richard Wright, whose novels portray
     only western culture. Hughes, on the contrary, balances
     the two perspectives. See also 1968.B15.

6   PARKER, JOHN W. Review of The Best of Simple, CLAJ, 5
     (December), 155-157.
          The Best of Simple does not so much extend the Simple
     tradition as collect choice pieces from Simple Speaks His
     Mind, Simple Takes a Wife, and Simple Stakes a Claim. A
     preponderance comes from the middle book. The new volume
     indicates both change and continuity: Hughes's forsaking
     poetry for prose, but maintaining Simple, who has enhanced
     his reputation during the last decade. Perhaps Simple is
     the "best-known fictional character in contemporary litera-
     ture." The illustrations here first appeared in the German
     edition of Simple Speaks His Mind. The Best of Simple
     shows Hughes's skill in handling humor and his mastery of
     simple narrative.

*7   WAGNER, JEAN. "Langston Hughes," Information and Documents,
     No. 135, Paris (January 15), pp. 30-35.
          Unlocatable. Cited in O'Daniel, 1971.A2.

1962 A BOOKS - NONE

1962 B SHORTER WRITINGS

1   BROWN, DEMING. "Other Opinions of the Nineteen Thirties,"
     in Soviet Attitudes Toward American Writing. Princeton:
     University Press.
          Since this decade, Hughes has been the most popular
     Negro writer. His pieces were judged not in terms of

1962

verisimilitude but in terms of their tendency to arouse
revolutionary action.

2   DILLARD, IRVING. "A Poet Asks: How Long Is a While?" SatR,
     45 (September 29), 32-33.
         Review of Fight for Freedom: The Story of the NAACP.
     Hughes speaks for the freedom riders and knows what he
     writes about. In Lawrence, Kansas, he could neither go to
     the movies nor buy an ice cream soda. He could not swim at
     the YMCA. Hughes will help make more meaningful the bi-
     centennial of the Emancipation Proclamation. Somebody
     should put this book in every library in the country.

3   FORD, NICK AARON. "Search for Identity: A Critical Survey of
     Significant Belles Lettres By and About Negroes Published
     in 1961," Phylon, 23, No. 2 (Summer), 138.
         On Ask Your Mama. Those who like Blues poetry will find
     pleasure in another display of Hughes's specialty. Others
     who have not accepted this kind of writing as legitimate
     poetry will sigh for the return of such moods as that of
     "The Negro Speaks of Rivers," "Let America Be America
     Again," and even "Brass Spitoons."

4   KIHSS, PETER. "Justice Comes High," NYTBR (September 2),
     p. 12.
         On Fight for Freedom. The facts and incidents are
     dramatic, and Hughes tells the story plainly.

1963 A BOOKS - NONE

1963 B SHORTER WRITINGS

1   ANON. "Biography and Memoirs," Book Week (October 27), p. 4.
         The Big Sea tells of life in Paris and Harlem during
     the 1920's. The first volume of the poet-author's auto-
     biography was originally published in 1940.

2   LEE, ULYSSES. Review of Ask Your Mama, CLAJ, 6, No. 3
     (March), 225-226.
         The book resembles the dozens. The tone is incisive,
     the humor biting. Even when it borders upon the shocking,
     the volume is clever and funny.

3   LONG, RICHARD A. Review of Something in Common and Other
     Stories, CLAJ, 7, No. 2 (December), 177.
         Hughes demonstrates his ability to handle many styles
     and moods. The stories written in the urban Negro idiom,

of which Hughes is the undisputed master, are by far the
best. "Father to Son," is a cornerstone in his work. Some
stories, however, rely too heavily on a surprise ending;
others show a "strange ineptness" of dialogue or
characterization.

4   _____. Review of Poems from Black Africa, CLAJ, 7, No. 2
     (December), 177.
         The panorama interests one. The poets especially worth
     mentioning in the English language group are Abioseh Nicol,
     Sierra Leone; Gabriel Okara, Nigeria; and E. K. Parks,
     Ghana. Of the French group, Senghor is probably repre-
     sented most. The usefulness of the oral verse is dubious.
     The volume displays the African sensibility more than it
     presents a "highly artistic achievement."

5   MORSE, CARL. "All Have Something to Say," NYTBR (October 6),
     p. 8.
         Hughes is a sharp reminder that good poetry lies not in
     literary influences or in literary schools but in the
     "private and personal accomplishment" of individuals.

6   NICHOLS, LEWIS. "Poems to Play: Langston Hughes Describes
     the Genius of His Tambourines to Glory," NYT (Sunday,
     October 3), Sect. II, Drama, p. 3.
         Joel Scheker and associates are the producers...such
     players as Hilda Simms are in the cast, and Tambourines
     will present the oddity of being one of the few nointe-
     grated shows in town.

7   PRESLEY, JAMES. "The American Dream of Langston Hughes,"
     SWR, 48 (Autumn), 380-386.
         Reaction to the American Dream has been one of Hughes's
     most recurring themes. Three strains--Indian, Negro, and
     Caucasian--contributed to his bloodlines of slaves, warriors,
     and planters. "Let America Be America Again" and "Freedom's
     Plow," two verses, especially reflect his motif. Of
     Hughes's prose, the Simple tales elaborate the "most tell-
     ing criticism of racial discrimination." In Not Without
     Laughter Sandy views the dream as Hughes had. If the real
     Hughes saw the evil behind this dream, he still knew of the
     good there.

8   TURPIN, WALTER. Review of Five Plays by Langston Hughes,
     CLAJ, 7, No. 2 (December), 180-181.
         This collects Hughes's dramas under one cover for the
     first time. The format and general publishing are of high
     quality.

41

1964

1964 A BOOKS

1   DICKINSON, DONALD C. A Bio-Bibliography of Langston Hughes.
    Hamden: Archon Books.
        The book has two divisions: biography and bibliography.
    The first has several chapters: I. "Early Years, 1902-
    1925"; II. "Harlem Renaissance, 1926-1930"; III. "Prose
    and Poetry of Protest"; and IV. "Mature Years, 1941-1963."
    This first section also has an "Introduction" and "Conclu-
    sion." The second section provides an explanation to the
    bibliography and these listings: primary works; editions;
    book-length translations; foreign works to which no English
    translation exists; prose and drama; and selected reviews
    of major works. Slight revisions for the 1967 and 1972
    editions occur. See 1965.B1.

*2   QUINOT, RAYMOND. Langston Hughes. Bruxelles: Editions CELF.
    Listing and book unlocatable.

1964 B SHORTER WRITINGS

1   CAMPBELL, FRANCIS D. Review of Simple's Uncle Sam, LJ, 90
    (November 1), 4806.
        Although Hughes demonstrates a sensitive wit throughout
    the book, his pieces are a light-hearted approach to the
    color problem in America. Hughes's greatest accomplishment
    lies in his "bringing the white man to Harlem and not
    vice-versa."

2   CUBAN, LARRY. The Negro in America. Glenview: Scott,
    Foresman, and Company, pp. 109-110.
        Hughes believed that a writer should recreate what he
    knows best, and he identified with the Negro masses. By
    artistic skill, he combined racial pride and created mili-
    tant literature typical of the Harlem Renaissance.

3   JACKSON, IRMA WERTZ. "Profile: Langston Hughes," NHB, 27
    (March), 146-147.
        Hughes's poems have been translated into more than
    twenty-five different languages, including Hindi, Gujarati,
    and Bengalese, as well as the more popular German, French,
    and Spanish. He ranks among the "most prolific and versa-
    tile writers of the Twentieth Century." The world has
    taught him, and his writings breathe the understanding that
    is necessary for brotherhood and peace. His African Treas-
    ury gives the American public a brilliant sampling of
    literature from the Continent. Of his characters, Jesse B.
    Semple makes him immortal.

4   JACOBS, LELAND. "Langston Hughes," <u>Instructor</u> (March), pp.
    116-117.
        Hughes's lyrics attract children. In "Time of Silver
    Rain," "Mexican Market Woman," and "Proposition," Hughes
    offers effective techniques that appeal: painted images,
    verbal designs, and sound patterns. Hughes helps readers,
    young and old, to feel the vibrancy of the human spirit.

5   O'DANIEL, THERMAN B. "Lincoln's Man of Letters," <u>LUB</u>:
    <u>Langston Hughes Issue</u>, pp. 9-12.
        In literature Hughes has achieved distinction. He has
    shown us what talent can achieve, even in an unfriendly
    society. In America today he is one of the most indus-
    trious and prolific writers. This is the original copy
    for the introduction to O'Daniel's book, 1971.A2.

6   SCHLEIFER, MARC. "Sepia Deb Ball," <u>The Nation</u>, 198 (June),
    665-666.
        Review of <u>New Negro Poets, USA</u>. Gwendolyn Brooks does
    the introduction, since Hughes does not do his own.

7   SPENSER, T. J. and CLARENCE J. RIVERS. "Langston Hughes: His
    Style and Optimism," <u>DC</u>, 7 (Spring), 99-103.
        Hughes's race and idiom are two reasons for his relative
    obscurity. So is his failure to innovate. Being at the
    "mercy of circumstances," the Simple of the drama is not
    the Simple of the short fiction. Not having a style in a
    structural way, Hughes has one in the "more inclusive sense
    of a controlling manner of thought." The latter makes him
    important as a playwright. When dealing with his charac-
    ters, white and black, Hughes has honesty and tolerance.
    In the sense of "advocating a cause," or limiting his
    audience, Hughes has never been a Negro playwright.

1965 A BOOKS - NONE

1965 B SHORTER WRITINGS

1   DICKINSON, DONALD CHARLES. "A Bio-Bibliography of Langston
    Hughes," <u>DA</u> (University of Michigan), 25 (May), 1282.
        Most of Hughes's early verse features two themes: pride
    in the Negro race and protest against white misunderstand-
    ing and hate. Socialistic dogma burdens the verses of the
    1930's. During the 1940's and 1950's, Hughes succeeded in
    using different forms. Except for passing mention, liter-
    ary critics and historians have neglected him. Expanded
    1964.A1. The formats of both are the same.

1965

2   FARRISON, W. EDWARD. Review of Simple's Uncle Sam, CLAJ, 9
     (September 1965-March 1966), 296-300.
         Here, more often than in earlier volumes, Hughes is too
     serious to laugh, too philosophical to cry. He can do no
     more than smile sardonically. Simple's account of a coffee-
     break conversation between him and his white boss is ingen-
     ious. Comparing Simple with Paul Bunyan or Davy Crockett
     is inappropriate, since both are legendary, or partly so.
     Comparisons with Mr. Dooley are more appropriate, since
     both comment on affairs of the times. Simple's dialect,
     however, is "more natural than Dooley's mutilated English."

3   GLOSTER, HUGH M. Negro Voices in American Fiction. New York:
     Russell and Russell, pp. 219-222.
         Reprint of 1948.B2.

4   POORE, CHARLES. "Books of the Times," NYT (Thursday,
     November 11), p. 45.
         Review of Simple's Uncle Sam. Hughes is an expert on
     satire. Having delighted one generation, his character
     Simple now delights another. Simple is a Harlem philosopher
     who illuminates simple morality.

5   ROLLINS, CHARLEMAE HILL. Famous American Negroes. New York:
     Dodd Mead, pp. 69-74.
         Hughes is "one of the best known and best loved poets
     in America." Since his verses appeal to the young as well
     as to the old, he is a poet for all. In a style quite
     different from that of Dunbar, he has captured the flavor
     of Negro speech.

1966 A BOOKS - NONE

1966 B SHORTER WRITINGS

1   DAVIS, ARTHUR P. "The Harlem of Langston Hughes's Poetry,"
     in Images of the Negro in American Literature. Edited by
     Seymour L. Gross and John Edward Hardy.
         Reprint of 1952.B5.

2   EMANUEL, JAMES A. "The Short Stories of Langston Hughes,"
     DA (Columbia University) 27 (July), 474-475A.
         Hughes's sixty-five short stories, relatively unknown
     and unstudied, entertain and have meaning. Often this
     meaning is obvious but symbolic. The author merges pic-
     ture and idea in images of song, weariness, and crucifix-
     ion. Other images such as snow, metal, and laughter,

function similarly. Hughes's weaknesses concern occasional didacticism and nonindividualized speech. From his pen, sentence fragments, parentheses, and explanations rarely come easily and clearly. The best five stories are "Father and Son," "Little Dog," "Cora Unashamed," "Big Meeting," and "On the Road." Expanded 1967.A1.

3   LITTLEJOHN, DAVID. <u>Black on White: A Critical Survey of Writing by American Negroes</u>. New York: Viking Press, pp. 51-55, 144-147.
      The value of <u>Not Without Laughter</u>, like that of Du Bois's social essays, lies in its completeness, truth, control, and wide humanity. "It is probably the most genuine inside view of Negro life available in the fiction of the period." The tone has a touch of sadness but never violence or bitterness. Although it is emotionally moving, the work avoids false sentiment. It is very small, "really," in outline but the stories have the warmth and genuineness of life.

<u>1967 A BOOKS</u>

1   EMANUEL, JAMES A. <u>Langston Hughes</u>. New York: Twayne Publishers.
      Chapters are as follows: "Big Sea"; "Cult of the Negro"; "Christ and the Killers"; "Love, Life, and Negro Soul"; and "A Wheel in Harlem." The work has some notes and references, a selected bibliography, and an index. Primary listings include books, uncollected pieces, and interviews. Secondary listings include books and articles.
      Hughes was the "dean of Negro writers in America." He crossed the desert with Arthur Koestler and chatted with Boris Pasternak. This Harlem writer found therapeutic value in the sea. He constantly returned to the theme that Negro hope is the miracle of American history, for this hope exists despite inhumanity. Hughes's Blues poems contribute a new form to our literature. Concerning American Négritude, Hughes is most representative because he emphasizes racial durability and the recognition of an African heritage. This strain found its strongest expression during his early years when he portrayed Negroes' "historical consciousness of their American past." "Mulatto" is his best poem, but he has written a score that deserve critical scrutiny. Expanded version of 1966.B2.

1967

1967 B SHORTER WRITINGS

1   ANON. "The Death of Simple," <u>Newsweek</u>, 69 (June 5), 104.
        He was born with rhythm. In the early thirties, he was
    involved with causes such as that of the Scottsboro boys;
    in the late forties, he experienced the bigotry of black-
    lists. In recent years he belonged to the past more than
    to the present. His gentle voice was almost inaudible in
    the sound and fury that occurred when Watts burned to ashes.

2   ANON. "Farewell to Langston Hughes," <u>Crisis</u>, 74 (June)
    252-254.
        At the age of 65, Hughes died on May 22 in Polyclinic
    Hospital in New York City. With compassion, humor, and
    love, he wrote of the common people.

3   ANON. "Hughes at Columbia," <u>New Yorker</u>, 43 (December 30), 21.
        The students and faculty of Hughes's first university
    meet to have a program, "A Langston Hughes Memorial Eve-
    ning." Professor Shenton, who must leave early, confesses:
    "I am here partly as a way of saying for Columbia that we
    owe some apologies...For a while, there lived a poet down
    the street from Columbia and Columbia never took the time
    to find out what he was about."

4   ANON. "Langston Hughes Dies at 65: Noted Poet and Playwright,"
    <u>NHB</u>, 30 (October) 16.
        Hughes had remained a writer of protest, crying out
    against the Negro's condition, but he never became embit-
    tered. His work never showed hatred or venom.

5   ANON. "Langston Hughes: Poet Laureate Graces Los Angeles,"
    <u>Sepia</u>, 16 (June), 55-59.
        Hughes's social criticism is as potent today as yester-
    day. The Harlem writer will read and lecture during Negro
    History week.

6   ANON. "NAACP Mourns Hughes," <u>NYAN</u> (27 May), p. 29.
        Hughes won the love of his people by his richness of
    cheer and compassion, and by his "righteous indignation
    over wrongs."

7   ANON. "Obituary Notes," <u>Publisher's Weekly</u>, 191, No. 24
    (June), 37.
        Hughes was unlike the generation that came after him.
    His approach was more wry than angry, more sly than mili-
    tant. During the McCarthy era he was labeled a Communist
    and certain of his books were censored, removed from U.S.
    Information Libraries overseas.

*8   BROOKS, GWENDOLYN. "He Knew the Street," CDN, (June 3).
      Unlocatable. See reprint (1970.B2) for annotation.

9   ____. "Langston Hughes," The Nation, 205, 7.
      Hughes had an affectionate interest in the young. He
      captured the heart of the street and its people.

10   BURROUGHS, MARGARET. "Langston Hughes Lives," ND, 16
      (September), 59-60.
      Hughes possessed a "rare creative soul." He consis-
      tently encouraged others.

11   DIAKHATÉ, LAMINE. "Langston Hughes, Conquérant de l'espoir,"
      PA, 64, 38-42.
      Hughes was a pilgrim who affirmed the identity of man in
      the face of the absurd. He showed the problems of Blacks
      in a democratic society; he restored to honor the rhythmical
      language of Africa that jazz introduced in America. Hughes
      was a man of the multitude, and a carrier of the hope that
      is inextinguishable.

12   DODAT, FRANÇOIS. "Situation de Langston Hughes," PA, 64,
      47-50.
      Until his last breath, he kept an optimism rooted in an
      "inalterable fois en l'homme." He rejected the submissive
      attitude of Booker T. Washington, but failed to adopt the
      "revolutionary conclusions of Malcom X." His purpose was
      to direct readers and listeners to a high level from which
      they could contemplate the "longue and douloureuse histoire
      d'un peuple." Since childhood, music has inspired Hughes's
      poetry and acts. In jazz he mingles with the people of his
      ancestors. Deep-seated generosity was the most striking
      trait of his life and work. "Son role n'était pas de
      diriger le combat, mais de décrire la Terre Promise."

13   EMANUEL, JAMES A. "Soul in the Works of Langston Hughes," ND,
      16 (September), 25-30, 74-92.
      Reprinted from 1967.A1.

14   EVANS, MARI. "I Remember Langston," ND, 16 (September), 36.
      Hughes was "the most generous professional I have ever
      known." His work inspired me as a poet, and I thought him
      "the most important influence of our time."

15   FARRISON, W. EDWARD. Review of The Best Short Stories of
      Negro Writers, CLAJ, 10, No. 4 (June), 358.
      This is the work of a well-established author, antholo-
      gist, and editor.

1967

16 _____. Review of The Book of Negro Humor, CLAJ, 10
(September–June), 72–74.
The Book of Negro Humor is both a novel and new addi-
tion to Hughes's already varied list of anthologies. In
insight and humor, selections from Simple "rank among the
best."

17 FIELDS, JULIA. "The Green of Langston's Ivy," ND, 16
(September), 58–59.
Hughes is not only a great poet, but a "great human
being." He respected the literary efforts of the young
and bridged the gulf of generations.

18 GAYLE, ADDISON, JR. "Langston Hughes: A Simple Commentary,"
ND, 16 (September), 53–57.
Like Wright, Hughes was a Negro writer and, like Wright,
he never denied it. His message of a people has kept his
work alive, but few people read him. Because high schools
and colleges sustain literary reputations over the long run,
posterity will escape him.

19 GUILLÉN, NICHOLÁS. "Le Souvenir de Langston Hughes," PA, 64,
34–37.
Being a mulatto, he doubted that he inspired confidence
in the masses, the recipients of his service and struggle.
From the first to the last, his poetry has concerned the
Black effort in North America. As such, it merits the
deepest respect.

20 JONES, ELDRED. "Laughing to Keep from Crying," PA, 64, 51–55.
This title symbolizes Hughes's spirit. His character
Simple embodies the American Negro problem and his bitter-
sweet humor. If one can read only one of the author's
works, it should be The Best of Simple. Hughes bridged
young and old; America and Africa; black and white.

21 KATZ, BILL. Review of The Panther and the Lash: Poems of Our
Times, LJ, 92 (June), 2164.
Hughes's style swings and mocks. He has been in the
process of writing another version of Ginsberg's Kaddish
for some thirty years and deserves more attention. He con-
forms neither to liberal nor to reactionary views of
Negroes.

22 KINNAMON, KENETH. "The Man Who Created Simple," The Nation,
205 (December 4), 599–601.
Much of his enormous volume of work is hack, but by his
pen and his appearances on platforms, he supported himself

for thirty-seven years: "No other serious Negro writer
survived so long and did so much in an often unreceptive
literary marketplace." Hughes aided other Negro writers
in many ways, since Poetry of the Negro introduced Robert
Hayden and Owen Dodson. Although many of Hughes's recent
poems catch the tone of black retribution, the earlier verse
more often depicts the Negro as passive victim, as in "Christ
in Alabama," and "Jim Crow Car." Unlike LeRoi Jones and
his generation, Hughes never relinquished the "dream of
racial fraternity, even in the deep South." That he chose
to end The Panther and the Lash with "Daybreak in Alabama"
affirms this. Surviving from 1930 to 1963, such hope may
now be all but dead among Negro writers. The Panther and
the Lash reminds us that since 1926 (The Weary Blues)
Hughes has mirrored the Negro mood. Time did not improve
his poetry.

*23 LUCAS, BOB. "The Poet Who Invented Soul," Los Angeles
       Sentinel (June 8), p. D-1.
            Unlocatable. Cited in O'Daniel, 1971.A2.

24 MAYFIELD, JULIAN. "Langston," ND, 16 (September), 34-35.
          He spent a disproportionate time of his working life
      helping young writers "get a foot in the door."

25 MITCHELL, LOFTEN. Black Drama. New York: Hawthorn Books,
       pp. 97, 145-147, 204-205.
            Hughes's Prodigal Son opened at the Greenwich News
      Theater in May, 1965. Having run until September, it
      moved to Europe. Vinette Carol directed the play vividly
      and movingly. Rich in feeling, the play reminded one of
      Hughes's earlier success in Black Nativity. Few people
      in American letters capture the feelings of blacks as
      vividly as Hughes. His love of his race shows in his
      work. Tambourines to Glory was well done and often moving,
      but the critics disliked it.

26 _____. "In Memoriam to a Beloved Friend," NYAN (27 May),
       pp. 1, 29.
            Hughes helped black writers more than anyone can imagine.
      As a literary and human giant, he was a vital part of the
      Harlem Renaissance. I first met him when I was a boy in
      Harlem. I met him again in the nineteen thirties, when
      Harlem Suitcase Theater produced his play Don't You Want
      to Be Free. He read my work and sang its praises to pro-
      ducers. In the future, people will know Hughes as the man
      who capitalized [sic] Black letters.

1967

27   RANDALL, DUDLEY. "Three Giants Gone," ND, 16 (November), 87.
        Hughes's death in May, 1967 adds to the toll of M. B.
     Tolson's and Jean Toomer's in 1966. All wrote during the
     Negro Renaissance of the 1920's, and Hughes was one of the
     most prolific. His humor, themes, and forms have influenced
     many Negro writers. To expand traditional modes like the
     ballad or couplet, he created variation or syncopation.

28   TURPIN, WATERS E. "Four Short Fiction Writers of the Harlem
     Renaissance - Their Legacy of Achievement," CLAJ, 11
     (September), 64-67.
        Hughes's "Slave on the Block" is a penetrating and
     satirical portrait of arty and liberal whites.

29   WILKINS, ROY. "Langston Hughes: A Tribute," Crisis, 74
     (June), 246.
        Hughes's death deprives Negroes and Americans in general
     of some precious virtue that "eased many a weary period of
     their lives." He gave cheer and compassion.

1968 A BOOKS

1   MELTZER, MILTON. Langston Hughes: A Biography. New York:
     Thomas Y. Crowell.
        The sections are "Wandering"; "Brass Spittoon"; "Hurry
     Up: Hurry Up"; "I've Known Rivers"; "Columbia"; "Harlem";
     "Africa"; "A Garret in Paris"; "Busboy Poet"; "College Man";
     "Black Renaissance"; "Not Without Laughter"; "People Need
     Poetry"; "Jim Crow, Southern Style"; "Around the World";
     "Dream Deferred"; "Rehearsal"; "The Bloody Spanish Earth";
     "Theater in a Suitcase"; "Poems and Politics"; "Simple
     Speaks His Mind"; "I Used to Wander"; "Postscript"; and
     "Bibliography." This last section lists volumes of poems,
     short and long fiction, autobiography, drama, history, edi-
     tions, and translations. Hughes believed that good writing
     comes out of your own life. With the possible exception of
     eating, he liked nothing better than sleeping. If anything
     lasts, he will. He was like a diamond.

1968 B SHORTER WRITINGS

1   BONTEMPS, ARNA. "Langston Hughes: He Spoke of Rivers,"
     Freedomways, 8 (May), 140-143.
        Before he finished college, Hughes's personal history
     began to read like a legend. Everything that follows is
     in tune with his first poems. His repeated use of the word

soul in the refrain of "Rivers" represents the first contemporary usage of this term. Its connotation concerns a
"Negro" quality in American self-expression and culture.

2 BRITT, DAVID DOBBS. "The Image of the White Man in the Fiction of Langston Hughes, Richard Wright, James Baldwin,
and Ralph Ellison," DA (Emory University), 29 (October),
1532A.
    Hughes and Ellison surpass Wright and Baldwin by finding
in the Black community those values that the artist can
celebrate. Hughes is best in the vignette forms of poetry
and in short fiction.

3 CLARKE, JOHN HENRIK. "Langston Hughes and Jesse B. Semple,"
Freedomways, 8 (Spring), 167-169.
    Simple's comments on the world of Harlem and on his own
daily troubles distinguish him in Afro-American literature.
In a few sentences, he says more than some Ph.D. authori-
ties have said in a small mountain of books. He will probably "outlive the circumstances of his creation."

4 DAVIS, ARTHUR P. "Langston Hughes: Cool Poet," CLAJ, 11
(June), 280-296.
    Hughes never fanatically supported any cause. His verses
have categories: poems on and about Harlem; poems concerning the American Negro's African background; poems of protest and social commentary; poems based on influence by
folk material; and miscellaneous poems. Harlem is his
dominant theme. If the early verses about Africa are
childishly vague, the later ones are politically concrete.
Senghor found the most Négritude of any American poet in
Hughes. Cullen agonized over being Negro, but Hughes
accepted it and found glory. Hughes's The Panther and the
Lash is a "kind of testament of his social stand." Here he
approaches bitterness as much as ever. His work, studied
chronologically, is a more perceptive and meaningful commentary than a library of sociological works. Statement
more than symbol characterizes his verse, and he ignores
the "New Critics." As an American classic, Hughes will
outlast this century.

5 DICKINSON, DONALD C. "Langston Hughes and the Brownie's Book,"
NHB, 31 (December), 8-10.
    As managing editor, Jessie Fauset published some of
Hughes's poems after his graduation from Central High in
Cleveland and encouraged Hughes to send more samples of his
work. The Brownie's Book printed his poems and stories
but, more important, it brought him to the attention of the

1968

editorial staff of The Crisis where his adult verse began
to appear simultaneously. The early work shows the theme
of poverty among plenty, the motif developed in his adult
verse.

6   EMANUEL, JAMES. "A Critical Analysis," R&W, 7, No. 5, 38-39.
The West Illana stories (Emanuel's term) prefigure the
techniques of Hughes's later writings: expository passages,
mixed sentences, fragments, stops for exclamations, and
repetitions. "Bodies in the Moonlight" is the first of
sixty-six short narratives that Hughes wrote. See 1968.B9.

7   _____. Dark Symphony. New York: Free Press, pp. 196-200.
For more than forty-five years Hughes has been America's
senior man of professions. His purpose was to illuminate
the Negro condition in America. In the range of his creations, Simple is the one great character of fiction. Every
decade of Hughes's career demonstrates his lyricism. In some
stories his chief virtues overbalance slight characterization and didacticism: dialogue unerringly shaped to ca-
dences, accents and phrases familiar to most Negroes;
incident, personality, and racial history woven into
recurrent patterns; interspersed songs; realistic and
Chekhovian endings.

8   _____. "The Literary Experiments of Langston Hughes," CLAJ,
11, 335-344.
In 1961 Hughes was elected to the National Institute of
Arts and Letters. The distinction of The Panther and the
Lash concerns the reprinting of "Christ in Alabama," which
in 1931 nearly caused a riot. Revised (1971.B5).

9   _____. "The Short Fiction of Langston Hughes," Freedomways,
8, 170-178.
This condenses Emanuel's doctoral dissertation. As the
author of sixty-six short stories, Hughes deserves close
study. His interspersed songs and Chekovian endings en-
hance his style; they suggest racial history and modern
impasses in social progress. Using simple plots, Hughes
handles flashbacks with grace. By rarely attempting to
round out his characters, he develops only a few: Cora
Jenkins, Mrs. Lloyd, Oceola Jones, Clara Briggs, Colonel
Norwood, Carl Anderson, Professor Brown, Charlie Lee, and
Flora Bell Yates. Despite claims to the contrary, his
characters are well-balanced. In his first two collections,
only two figures are bitter: Bert of "Father to Son" and
Charlie Lee of "Powder White Faces." See also 1966.B2;
1968.B6.

10   FARRISON, W. EDWARD. Review of The Panther and the Lash,
        CLAJ, 3 (March), 259-261.
            Hughes prepared this collection, which was in press when
        he died. All are poems of the times, since they pertain to
        the Negro's continuing struggle for first-class citizenship
        in America. "Backlash Blues" is said to be the last verse
        that Hughes submitted before he died.

11   _____. Review of Sweet Flypaper of Life, CLAJ, 11, No. 2
        (March), 261-263.
            This new edition of the book, which first appeared in
        1955, is reprinted from a personal copy of the first edi-
        tion. Before he died, Hughes gave the latter to the pub-
        lishers. De Carva's photographs excel, but Sister Mary
        Bradley's monologue adds what photography alone cannot
        communicate.

12   HOLMES, EUGENE C. "Langston Hughes: Philosopher Poet,"
        Freedomways, 8 (Spring), 144-151.
            Hughes was one of the "best-rounded and most multi-
        faceted men of his time." He was a philosopher because
        he developed a Weltanschauung, a cultural pluralism and
        commonality that endure. Like Sterling Brown, he was con-
        cerned with a re-evaluation of the Negro folk. Of all the
        poets in the Negro Renaissance, he alone achieved maturity.
        He proposed not an art for art's sake, but an art for
        people's sake.

13   HUDSON, THEODORE R. "Langston Hughes' Last Volume of Verse,"
        CLAJ, 11 (June), 345-48.
            In The Panther and the Lash Hughes tries too hard and
        forces his verses. At times one finds the prosaic rather
        than the poetic, and the result is that the verses stimu-
        late the mind, if not the heart. As in some of his earlier
        poems of protest, he sacrifices the poetic touch to grim
        sincerity. He "disclaims rather than sings."

14   JACKSON, BLYDEN. "A Word About Simple," CLAJ, 11, No. 2,
        (June), 338-343.
            With the portrait of Simple, Hughes explores what
        Negroes are really like. The character is an "ordinary
        person who is a Negro." Having come from Virginia, Simple
        departs from Negro stereotypes. He is an unpolished dia-
        mond. Reprinted in 1970.B5; 1971.A2.

15   JAHN, JANHEINZ. Neo-African Literature: A History of Black
        Writing. New York: Grove Press, pp. 194-198.

1968

    Langston Hughes and Richard Wright are the most important writers of two different schools. Wright rejects the African heritage in order to be universal, but succeeds only when placing a problem in a local and particular context. By stressing the folklorist element, however, Hughes achieves universal influence and status. Hughes preferred the Afro-American cultural heritage to any ideology. From his first poems, one can see exoticism and anti-bourgeois identification.

16   JONES, HARRY L. "A Danish Tribute to Langston Hughes," CLAJ, 11 (June), 331-334.
    Simple is as much Dane as Negro, for he is every little man who perceives the discrepancy between society's preachments and its practices. From the subject of race, Hughes moves to the universal problem of human suppression. He makes us aware that it is no tragedy to be Negro, but a shame to be white.

17   KAISER, ERNEST. "Selected Bibliography of the Published Writings of Langston Hughes," Freedomways, 8 (Spring), 85-191.
    This listing has five sections: Introduction; Books and Pamphlets (authored, edited, or translated singly or jointly), 64 entries; Introductions and Chapters in Books, 13 entries; Magazine articles by, 14 entries; Magazine and Newspaper articles, 12 entries. With one exception, this bibliography omits works written in foreign languages. It does, however, give biographical information. Hughes lacked the "rhetorical heights and lyrical intensity" of a W. E. B. Du Bois, Richard Wright, or James Baldwin. He was, nevertheless, talented, versatile, and prolific. Among Black writers, his bibliography is second only to that of Du Bois.

18   KRAMER, AARON. "Robert Burns and Langston Hughes," Freedomways, 8 (Spring), 159-166.
    Both poets experienced poverty and hopelessness as children. They were nurtured on the songs and legends, the frustration and fury, of a nation enslaved by a great power. At the moment of cultural renaissance for his people, each writer came to manhood. Each sought nondialect excellence and fame within the literary circles of the "master race," but preferred his own folk tradition.

19   MARGOLIES, EDWARD. Native Sons: A Critical Survey of Twentieth Century American Authors. Philadelphia and New York: J. P. Lippincott, pp. 35-38.

Hughes is the most popular writer to come out of the Harlem Renaissance. His free verse belongs to the tradition of Whitman, Lindsay, and Sandburg. As a folk artist he writes "for the people he is writing about."

20 MATHEUS, JOHN F. "Langston Hughes as Translator," CLAJ, 11 (June), 319-330.
    See reprint (1971.B14) for annotation.

21 MITCHELL, LOFTEN. "For Langston Hughes and Stella Holt," ND, 17 (April), 41-43, 74-77.
    The two never belittled other Blacks. Hughes passed writing assignments on to others. He wrote "better than Hollywood and Broadway combined."

22 O'DANIEL, THERMAN B. "Langston Hughes: A Selected Classified Bibliography," CLAJ, 11 (June), 349-366.
    Reprints and expands 1951.B4. Reprinted and expanded in 1971.B16.

23 PATTERSON, LINDSAY. "Langston Hughes - An Inspirer of Young Writers," Freedomways, 8, 179-181.
    Hughes did more than inspire; he cared about the writer and the work. I dedicated my first book, Anthology of the Negro in the American Theater, to him. But the day that it came was the day that he died.

24 SMALLEY, WEBSTER. "Introduction," in Five Plays by Langston Hughes. Bloomington: Indiana University Press, pp. xii-xviii.
    The text of Mulatto, Hughes's first professionally produced play, appears for the first time in this volume. This drama is the only one here in which a white character is more than peripheral. In other plays in which white characters occur, they are little more than symbols of evil, good, or indifference. Hughes does not always create a serious tone. His folk plays are simultaneously humorous and revealing. For the definitive folk comedy of life in Harlem, one can cite Simply Heavenly. Among Hughes's comedies, however, Tambourines to Glory is most serious and dramatic.

25 TURNER, DARWIN T. "Langston Hughes as Playwright," CLAJ, 11 (June), 297-309.
    See Reprint (1971.B17) for annotation.

1969 A BOOKS - NONE

1969

1969 B SHORTER WRITINGS

1   ANON. Review of Black Magic, AtlM, 224 (August), 103.
    These juvenile miseries are variations of the affronts
    to self-esteem that all children suffer. The pieces are
    more amusing than tragic.

2   BRAWLEY, BENJAMIN. The Negro Genius. New York: Biblo and
    Tanner, pp. 246-250.
    Whatever Hughes's shortcomings, he has been honest. He
    has adhered to his point of view and emphasized the racial
    idea. It would be better if Fine Clothes to the Jew had
    never been published; no other volume "reflects more
    fully the abandon and the vulgarity of its age."

3   COOK, MERCER and STEPHEN E. HENDERSON. The Militant
    Writer. Madison: The University of Wisconsin Press,
    pp. 102-107.
    Hughes was not only the poet; he was the "living source
    of his own resurrection in others." He was the most repre-
    sentative and most prolific of the New Negroes.

4   FARRISON, W. EDWARD. Review of Black Magic, CLAJ, 13
    (September), 87-88.
    The statements in Black Magic are so simple, informal,
    and compact as to be naive. To discerning readers, how-
    ever, they suggest more than they say explicitly. The book
    is a "new and challenging reminder" to those who believe in
    American democracy.

5   GRAVES, ELIZABETH MINOT. "A Selected List of Children's
    Books," CW (November 21), p. 259.
    On Black Magic. In a few lines and some telling drawings,
    this prose poem "drives home the heartache of growing up
    black in White America."

6   JOHNSON, LEMUEL A. The Devil, The Gargoyle, and The Buffoon.
    Port Washington: Kennikat Press, pp. 109-127.
    Hughes's The Weary Blues transforms a primitive expres-
    sion of the plantation into a new statement of exile in an
    urban setting. His attitude differs from that of Césaire
    in Cahier d'un Retour au Pays Natal and from the "polemic
    power and anger" of Guillién in West Indies. The two modes
    of The Weary Blues are jazz and blues. In the title poem,
    a disembodied and orphic voice sings with "soul-atrophying
    weariness."

7   MELTZER, MILTON. "Four Who Locked Horns with the Censors"
    [Hughes, Twain, Child and Sanger], <u>WLB</u>, 44 (November),
    279-280.
        Not a poet to write about abstract emotions, Hughes
    wrote about love--but love in Harlem. Since many of his
    poems were social, he persisted in telling the truth. In
    March of 1953, he was summoned before the McCarthy commit-
    tee, and his lecturing declined for a long time.

8   MINTZ, LAWRENCE E. "Langston Hughes's Jesse B. Semple: The
    Urban Negro as Wise Fool," <u>SN</u>, 7 (Fall), 11-21.
        Hughes uses humor as a weapon. While ridiculing the
    enemies of Blacks, he criticizes Blacks themselves. With
    realism, he portrays the daily life of the Black community.
    For his militancy, as well as his realism, Whites and Blacks
    alike condemned him. Hughes uses the technique of malaprop-
    ism, and one may categorize virtually all of the sketches
    in terms of race or women.

9   MITCHELL, LOFTEN. "That Other Man," <u>Crisis</u>, 77-78 (February),
    75-77.
        Hughes was a bigger man than I shall ever be. Since he
    was incredible, you do not describe him.

10 NOWER, JOYCE. "Foolin' Master," <u>SN</u>, 7 (Fall), 11-21.
        Hughes is part of the long tradition of fooling whites.
    In the Simple tales, he satirizes those Negroes who climb
    up the ladder and assume the middle class standards of the
    master who is pompous.

11 PRESLEY, JAMES. "Langston Hughes: A Personal Farewell," <u>SWR</u>,
    54 (Winter), 79-84.
        Although I was white and Texan, he touched my life. My
    being nearly thirty years his junior did not matter. From
    Ernest Hemingway and William Faulkner, his career stretched
    to Richard Wright, John Steinbeck, and Norman Mailer.
    Hughes did not touch the militant generation that called
    him old-fashioned. Whatever the form, he remained the
    poet of the people. For him, humor was a weapon against
    social prejudice, and Simple was possibly his finest crea-
    tion. To one or two generations of bigoted Americans, he
    was the radical agitator who went to Russia. There, with
    a Negro company, he was supposed to film <u>Porgy and Bess</u>.
    During the McCarthy era, this trip became a basis for ob-
    jecting to his work.

12 PROWLE, ALLEN D. "Langston Hughes," in <u>The Black American
    Writer</u>, Vol. 2. Edited by C. W. E. Bigsby, Deland,
    Florida: Everett/Edwards, pp. 78-86.

1969

> With varying degrees of intensity, Hughes expresses his
> dominant theme of protest which is always the basis of
> his creativity. Although feeling pessimistic at times, he
> was fundamentally an optimist. Ask Your Mama is a panorama
> of the deferred dream; it expresses Hughes's impatience to
> correct a situation that rarely changed during his lifetime.

13 SUTHERLAND, ZENA. "Reviewing Stand," SatR, 52 (August 16),
   27.
   > On Black Magic. Just before his death, Hughes wrote the
   > captions to this collection of sketches. Some of the work
   > has wry humor, but other parts have bitterness. All is
   > blunt.

14 TOPPIN, EDGAR A. A Biographical History of Blacks Since 1528.
   New York: David McKay, p. 327.
   > Over a forty-year career, Hughes was one of America's
   > finest and most versatile writers. Although generally con-
   > sidered to be the "Poet Laureate" of Blacks, he did more
   > than write great poetry; he did outstanding works in almost
   > every literary form. His first book, The Weary Blues
   > "vividly portrayed Negro urban folk life." Its verses
   > blended syncopated blues and jazz rhythms with black street
   > dialogue. Except for having a white patron, with whom he
   > broke in 1930, Hughes lived solely from his earnings as a
   > professional writer and reader of poetry.

1970 A BOOKS

1 MYERS, ELIZABETH P. Langston Hughes: Poet of His People.
  Champaign, Illinois: Garrard Publishing Company, 144 pp.
  > The chapters are as follows: "Earthquake"; "When You
  > Feel Like Crying"; "Laugh"; "The Salt of the Earth"; "A
  > Family for Langston"; "Central High School"; "Mexico
  > Again"; "Plans"; "Weary Blues"; "Launched on a Career";
  > "Not Without Laughter"; "Keep Your Hand on the Plow"; and
  > "Poet of His People."
  > Hughes responded to his grandmother's stories by dislik-
  > ing slavery. The old woman taught him to laugh when he
  > felt bad. Elected as class poet in the eighth grade, he
  > told his peers that all Negroes do not have rhythm. For
  > literary models, he took Paul Laurence Dunbar and Carl
  > Sandburg. During his years at Central High, he experienced
  > discrimination when looking for summer work. His father,
  > James Hughes, sneered at poor people; "Hurry Up!" was his
  > favorite phrase.

When feeling lonesome, Langston wrote poetry. In the
1920's he visited Marcus Garvey's headquarters. While in
Harlem, Hughes met Countee Cullen, who was a year his jun-
ior. He savored Du Bois's words to him: "The only thing
that matters, Mr. Hughes, is who and what you are and where
you stand. Never shrink from the truth." Hughes thought
that Garvey's movement was insensible.
On May 22, 1967 Hughes's death came unexpectedly and
after short illness. Vignette Carol, producer of his
Gospel play, Black Nativity, eulogized the writer. Hughes,
she said, "represented to countless Negroes a chance to
experiment and expand...to be just a little bit better than
we had dreamed possible."

2   ROLLINS, CHARLEMAE H. Black Troubador: Langston Hughes.
New York: Rand McNally, 143 pp.
    The chapters are as follows: "I've Known Rivers";
"Brand New Clothes"; "Gypsies Are Picture-Book People";
"Trip"; "College Formal"; "Renaissance Casino"; "Friendly
in a Friendly Way"; "The Troubador"; "Merry Go Round";
"Dear Lovely Death"; "Awards and Honors"; "Published Works";
and "Index." Plates of personages and letters occur.
    A moving description of a snowstorm by Maupassant in-
spired Hughes to write with exactness. Carl Sandburg,
Vachel Lindsay, and Amy Lowell had a profound effect upon
this black poet's career. Hughes saw Florence Mills, the
famous actress, perform in Shuffle Along. At Columbia
he missed a very important examination to attend the funeral of Bert Williams, the famous entertainer. While still
a young man, Hughes met many celebrities including W. E. B.
Du Bois, Countee Cullen, Walter White, Carl Van Vechten,
and H. L. Mencken. Hughes's best friend was Mary McLeod
Bethune who suggested that he give poetry readings throughout the country. In Russia Hughes met Arthur Koestler. At
Tuskegee Dr. Carver showed him a working laboratory.
    Hughes's work broke down racial barriers. Although not
a structured novel, Not Without Laughter has a development
of episode and character. In The Ways of White Folks, which
contains much of Hughes's best prose, "Cora Unashamed" is
powerfully moving. Although "Father to Son" is distinguished, Hughes was primarily a poet.

1970 B SHORTER WRITINGS

1   ANON. "A Note on Contempo and Langston Hughes," in Negro.
Edited by Nancy Cunard. New York: Frederick Ungar Publishing, p. 81.

1970

In December 1931, Hughes was on a lecture tour throughout the United States, and the students at Chapel Hill in-
vited him to speak. Contempo, a student publication,
printed the work of this writer who denounced the Scottsboro
case. The effect was of course "like wildfire."

2 BROOKS, GWENDOLYN. "Foreword," in Black Troubador: Langston
Hughes. New York: Rand McNally, pp. i-ii.
The works and deeds of Langston Hughes take root in
kindness. He began with a clarity of racial pride. When
the word "black" was less than a darling flag, he admired
it. He recognized the horror that men imposed upon each
other, but those who knew him will remember warm laughter.
He helped not only me, but hundreds: Frank London Brown,
Margaret Danner, Dudley Randall, Margaret Walker, Charlemae
Rollins, Ronald Fair, Eva Bell Thompson, Hoyt Fuller,
Conrad Kent Rivers, Margaret Taylor Burroughs, Lerone
Bennet, Jr., and Oscar Brown, Jr. See 1970.A2. Reprint
of 1967.B8.

3 DAVIS, ARTHUR P. "The Tragic Mulatto Theme in Six Works of
Langston Hughes," in Five Black Writers. Edited by
Donald B. Gibson. New York: University Press, pp. 167-177.
Reprint of 1955.B4.

4 DAVIS, CHARLES T. and DANIEL WALTER, eds. "Langston Hughes,"
in On Being Black. Greenwich: Fawcett, pp. 179-263.
Davis divides the book into four sections: "First
Stirrings"; "Coming of Age"; "Early Moderns"; and "Today
and Tomorrow." In the selections of poems from the nineteen twenties and thirties, Hughes is said to experiment
with "rhythms of Harlem speech, the feel of being black, and
the hope that springs eternal." In Montage of a Dream
Deferred, Hughes felt that he had introduced Bebop rhythms
and motifs into American poetry for the first time. As in
earlier poems, he portrayed the past and the South as well
as Harlem. The rhythms and changes in his poems parallel
the disorder of the communities that he knew. At the end
of the 1940's his voice was still a genuine reflection of
the Harlemite.

5 JACKSON, BLYDEN. "A Word About Simple," In Five Black Writers.
Edited by Donald B. Gibson. New York: University Press,
pp. 183-189.
Reprinted from 1968.B14; reprinted in 1971.A2.

6 MILES, WILLIAM. "Isolation in Langston Hughes," in Five Black
Writers. Edited by Donald B. Gibson. New York: University
Press, pp. 172-182.

The theme of Soul Gone Home is the isolation of Blacks
in an alien culture where they are forced to exist. Although a fantasy, both in situation and structure, the play
emphasizes the real circumstances of Black America. Two
incidents illustrate that the responsibility lies with the
white world: the complete indifference of white ambulance
drivers; the mother's symbolical whitening of face. Like
Wright, Hughes suggests that death alone provides "true
insight into the human condition." Since the social commentary is relevant to any oppressed minority, the play is
universal.

7   MILLER, JOHNINE BROWN. "The Major Theme in Langston Hughes's
    Not Without Laughter," CEA, 32, No. 6 (March), 8-10.
        Sandy will heal the split between the feminine world of
    feeling and materialism, and the masculine world of intel-
    lect and rational order. The first world is that of Hager
    and Harriett; the second, that of Tempy. By being Brown,
    Sandy is midway between his mother's blackness and his
    father's yellowness. Since she emulates whites, Tempy is
    not a suitable model for Sandy, but she does help him. By
    synthesizing the virtues of the other characters, Hager is
    as near a model as one can find in the novel.

8   WATKINS, CHARLES A. "Simple: The Alter Ego of Langston
    Hughes," Black Scholar, 2 (September), 18-26.
        Since there is nothing superhuman about the major char-
    acter, the Simple stories do not form an epic. For both
    Hughes and his black audience, the bourgeois interlocutor
    is a "moral negative."

9   WILLIAMS, J. KENNY. They Also Spoke: An Essay on Negro Lit-
    erature in America, 1787-1930. Nashville: Townsend
    Press, p. 268.
        Hughes was, by far, the most versatile poet of the
    Harlem Renaissance. He liberated himself from existing
    patterns of poetry, which he thought to be meaningless.
    To him, subject determined form, and his subjects exceeded
    the range of the traditional. He was realistic. Like
    James Weldon Johnson, he experimented with the Negro idiom,
    but he invoked the Blues rather than the nineteenth century
    preacher.

1971 A BOOKS

1   HAWTHORNE, LUCIA SHEILA. A Rhetoric of Human Rights as Ex-
    pressed in the "Simple Columns" by Langston Hughes.

1971

University Park of Pennsylvania: Doctoral Dissertation,
Pennsylvania State University, 206 pp.
From 1943 to 1966, Hughes wrote the "Simple Columns" in
the Chicago Defender. The pieces concerned probable results
of World War II, blatant racial injustice in the South and
North, the subway, minority groups, apartment living, education, traveling, colored hotels and restaurants, Othello
on Broadway, the NAACP, black pride and unity, Josephine
Baker, separation and divorce, and, finally, dealing with
the law. Some themes are especially prominent: racial
injustice; use of the term "black" as a substitute for
"colored" or "Negro"; importance of broader opportunities
in education, employment, and housing; language that fore-
shadows contemporary Black speech.

2   O'DANIEL, THERMAN B., ed. Langston Hughes: Black Genius.
New York: William Morrow, 241 pp.
The volume includes fourteen essays by scholars on
Hughes. Five of the articles appeared first in a special
issue on Langston Hughes, CLAJ, 11 (June, 1968).
The chapters are as follows: Therman B. O'Daniel,
"Langston Hughes" (1964.B5); Arthur P. Davis, "Langston
Hughes: Cool Poet" (1968.B4, 1971.B4); Nancy B. McGhee,
"Langston Hughes: Poet in the Folk Manner" (1971.B13);
Donald B. Gibson, "The Good Black Poet and the Good Gray
Poet: the Poetry of Hughes and Whitman" (1971.B9);
Darwin T. Turner, "Langston Hughes as Playwright" (1968.B25,
1971.B17); William Edward Farrison, "Not Without Laughter
But Without Tears" (1971.B7); Blyden Jackson, "A Word About
Simple" (1968.B14); Eugene W. Collier, "A Pain in His Soul:
Simple as Epic Hero" (1971.B3); Harry L. Jones, "Rhetorical
Embellishment in Hughes's Simple Stories" (1971.B10);
James A. Emanuel, "The Short Fiction of Langston Hughes"
(1968.B9); John F. Matheus, "Langston Hughes as Translator"
(1968.B20, 1971.B12); James A. Emanuel, "The Literary Ex-
periment of Langston Hughes" (1968.B8, 1971.B5); George E.
Kent, "Langston Hughes and Afro-American Folk and Cultural
Tradition" (1971.B11); Therman B. O'Daniel, "Langston Hughes:
A Selected Classified Bibliography" (1951.B4, 1968.B22,
1971.B16).

1971 B SHORTER WRITINGS

*1   BARISONZI, JUDITH ANNE. "Black Identity in the Poetry of
Langston Hughes," DA, 32, 3291A.
Cited in DA. Hughes's poetry shows a tension among
three alternatives that confront the Afro-American: integration, separatism or black nationalism, and radicalism.

It shows, too, a double consciousness between identification with the American mainstream and identification with
the ghetto.

2   CAREY, JULIAN C. "Jesse B. Semple Revisited and Revised,"
    <u>Phylon</u>, 32 (2nd Quarter), 158-163.
        Despite Joyce and the narrative "I" of the tales, Simple
    remains black. Sadie Maxwell Reaves, a resident of Sugar
    Hill, influences Joyce, and the "I" parrots the attitudes
    of the black bourgeoisie.

3   COLLIER, EUGENIA W. "A Pain in His Soul: Simple as Epic
    Hero," in <u>Langston Hughes: Black Genius</u>. Edited by
    Therman B. O'Daniel. New York: William Morrow, pp. 120-131.
        Twenty years after his literary birth in the <u>Chicago
    Defender</u> (1943), Simple had become the hero of the Black
    American epic. The narrative begins <u>in medias res</u>, since
    Simple is already an adult Harlemite.

4   DAVIS, ARTHUR P. "Langston Hughes: Cool Poet," in <u>Langston
    Hughes: Black Genius</u>. Edited by Therman B. O'Daniel.
    New York: William Morrow, pp. 18-38.
        Reprints 1968.B4.

5   EMANUEL, JAMES A. "The Literary Experiments of Langston
    Hughes," in <u>Langston Hughes: Black Genius</u>. Edited by
    Therman B. O''Daniel. New York: William Morrow, pp. 171-182.
        Literary experimentation characterized Hughes's career.
    <u>Ask Your Mama</u> has a technique that has outdistanced critical
    perceptions. Hughes's topographical and emblematic experi-
    ments have antecedents in seventeenth century England and
    America. This work ultimately relates to the acrostic verse
    of the early Greeks. In typography and exclamation, "The
    Cat and the Saxophone" (<u>The Weary Blues</u>) anticipates modes
    common to poets of the 1960's. In "Ballad of the Landlord"
    newspaper captions form lines of verse. The names of Harlem
    bars and nightclubs almost totally comprise "Neon Lights"
    (<u>Montage of a Dream Deferred</u>). "Elderly Leaders" and "Go
    Slow" fulfill technique that goes back to "The Cat and the
    Saxophone." Revises 1968.B8.

6   _____. "The Short Fiction of Langston Hughes," in <u>Langston
    Hughes: Black Genius</u>. Edited by Therman B. O'Daniel.
    New York: William Morrow, pp. 120-131.
        Reprints 1968.B9.

7   FARRISON, W. EDWARD. "Not Without Laughter But Without Tears,"
    in <u>Langston Hughes: Black Genius</u>. Edited by Therman B.
    O'Daniel. New York: William Morrow, pp. 96-109.

1971

<blockquote>

Not Without Laughter is an argument by narration, and
it appeals as much to the intellect and conscience as to
the emotions. Robert Bone may not know that the book was
in press before receiving its present title. Only Sandy
rivals Hager in vividness and interest. Sandy is the principal character, however, since he either causes action or
becomes the person whom it affects. Simplicity distinguishes
the writing.

</blockquote>

8   GARBER, EARLENE D. "Form as a Complement to Content in Three
of Langston Hughes's Poems," NALF 4 (Winter), 137-139.
When Paul Engle and Joseph Langland asked Hughes to sub-
mit a poem for Poet's Choice, he sent "Border Line." The
decision represents the concerns of his literary career.

9   GIBSON, DONALD B. "The Good Black Poet and the Good Gray
Poet: The Poetry of Hughes and Whitman," in Langston
Hughes: Black Genius. Edited by Therman B. O'Daniel.
New York: William Morrow, pp. 65-80.
Hughes comes within the Walt Whitman tradition. Not a
direct descendant, he was probably influenced more by Carl
Sandburg and Vachel Lindsay. Both Hughes and Whitman be-
lieve in the possible realization of the American ideal and
see America as in the process of becoming. Both were cheer-
ful more often than not, and furthered nontraditional uses
of form. Hughes, however, uses rhyme and traditional metrics more than Whitman. Although the two writers use personae, they are social poets rather than subjective ones.
Hughes remains optimistic throughout. Like Whitman, he was
completely engaged in his time, a man of the present and
future rather than the past. Critics attacked both writers
for their discussions about sex. Hughes, more than Whitman,
should be read aloud.

10 JONES, HARRY L. "Rhetorical Embellishment in Hughes's Simple
Stories," in Langston Hughes: Black Genius. Edited by
Therman B. O'Daniel. New York: William Morrow, pp. 132-144.
The Simple stories use the rhetorical devices developed
through the ages. Simple is a creation of his own words,
and within his world, one finds an opposition of embel-
lished and plain styles. The first produces humor, but the
second creates a tone of seriousness, honesty, and sincerity. In the tales, one finds three voices: Hughes's,
Boyd's, and Simple's. By being associated with the plain
style, Boyd functions as a straight man. He is less militant and more moderate than Simple. Rhyme is Hughes's most
obvious device of phonology. Other humorous effects occur:
malapropisms and wordplay; parallel pattering or parataxis,
and images.

11 KENT, GEORGE E. "Langston Hughes and Afro-American Folk and
    Cultural Tradition," in Langston Hughes: Black Genius.
    Edited by Therman B. O'Daniel. New York: William Morrow,
    pp. 183-210.
        One most appreciates Hughes's works by placing them in a
    folk and cultural tradition. If Western artists stress
    the timeless and universal, Hughes emphasizes the topical
    and the issues of the Black community. Not Without Laughter
    contains folk responses to existence, Blues, folk aphorisms,
    slave tall stories, dances, and spirituals. When at his
    best, Hughes attempts to capture the Blues spirit with non-
    Blues devices. His work shows the different and cultural
    modes of a religious tradition of spirituals, gospels, and
    sermons. Although he does not fully convert folk definitions
    into great art, he has tilled the ground for those who will
    follow.

12 McGHEE, NANCY B. "Langston Hughes: Poet in the Folk Manner,"
    in Langston Hughes: Black Genius. Edited by Therman B.
    O'Daniel. New York: William Morrow, pp. 39-64.
        Hughes created numerous characters of the folk style.
    Jesse B. Semple and Alberta K. Johnson are the most note-
    worthy of these. Hughes uses the traditions of Blues and
    jazz.

13 McPHERSON, JAMES M., et al. Blacks in America. Garden City:
    Doubleday.
        In paragraph form, this bibliography lists Hughes's
    major works from The Weary Blues to The Panther and the
    Lash. Nine secondary references are given; most signifi-
    cant are Emanuel (1967.A1) and Kramer (1968.B18).

14 MATHEUS, JOHN F. "Langston Hughes as Translator," in Langston
    Hughes: Black Genius. Edited by Therman B. O'Daniel. New
    York: William Morrow, pp. 157-170.
        Hughes's translation of "The Faithless Wife" is more
    accurate than the New Directions translation. In 1949,
    Hughes and Bontemps edited The Poetry of the Negro, 1746-
    1949, a work containing pieces written both in English and
    other languages. Hughes contributed eleven translations as
    well as fourteen original poems to this volume, three from
    French and eight from Spanish. His translation of
    Gabriela Mistral's Selected Poems is the "only translation
    of her works in book form." It includes seventy-four of
    her best poems. By helping Meyer Cook to revise Gouverneurs
    de la Rosée, Hughes passed the "supreme test of his transla-
    tive power." He showed himself a master of diction. He had
    a sense for Creole Patois and peasant speech. In Poems from
    Black Africa, he translated a French poem, "Flute Players"

1971

by Jean Joseph Rabearivelo, a famous poet of Madagascar.
Hughes translated into English two French poems by the
Sengalese David Diop, "Those Who Lost Everything" and "Suf-
fer, Poor Negro." Reprints 1968.B20.

15 O'DANIEL, THERMAN B. "Langston Hughes," in his Langston
    Hughes: Black Genius. New York: William Morrow, pp. 1-17.
        Hughes is one of the most talented and prolific writers
    in twentieth century America. At the time of his death
    The Panther and the Lash was in press. During a benefit
    and cabaret party sponsored by NAACP, Hughes met Walter
    White, Mary White Ovington, James Weldon Johnson, and Carl
    Van Vechten. The last helped Hughes to publish The Weary
    Blues. Simple is one of the most original characters in
    American literature. Hughes "never compromised his prin-
    ciples in order to produce a best seller." Reprints
    1964.B5.

16 _____. "Langston Hughes: A Selected Classified Bibliography,"
    in his Langston Hughes: Black Genius. New York: William
    Morrow, pp. 211-241.
        A general introduction outlines the scope and method.
    The primary listings are as follows: poetry, novels,
    children's story, autobiographies, biographies for young
    people, histories for young people, histories, translations,
    anthologies of his own writings, edited anthologies, full-
    length plays, one-act plays, gospel songs, Christmas cantata,
    lyrics for dramatic musicals, opera librettos, screen plays,
    radio scripts, and a few articles by Langston Hughes. Sec-
    ondary listings exist in two parts: "A few books and arti-
    cles about Langston Hughes" and "Reviews of Langston
    Hughes's books in the CLA Journal." Where feasible, all
    listings are chronological. Reprints and expands 1951.B4;
    1968.B22.

17 TURNER, DARWIN T. "Langston Hughes as Playwright," in Langston
    Hughes: Black Genius. Edited by Therman B. O'Daniel. New
    York: William Morrow, pp. 287-309.
        Despite extensive efforts, Hughes never became an out-
    standing dramatist. In order to assure that no one missed
    the point, he sometimes overstated it. Little Ham is
    slight and confused, heavily foreshadowed, and overly de-
    pendent upon chance and coincidence. In Don't You Want to
    Be Free, the scenes are predictable, but the narration
    effectively recounts historical Blacks who struggled for
    freedom: Nat Turner, Denmark Vessey, Harriet Tubman, and
    Sojourner Truth. There is an overemphasis on the proletarian
    theme of uniting workers, but the language and thought are

more artistic than that of any other play Hughes wrote.
The projection of a Negro audience, however, made it "un-
suitable for commercial production on Broadway." Often
Hughes created stereotypes. Too frequently, sentimentality
and fame detract from his characters. Emperor of Haiti and
Tambourines to Glory are his best plays. When writing
simply and lyrically, Hughes is most artistic. Reprints
1968.B25.

18   WALDRON, EDWARD E. "The Blues Poetry of Langston Hughes,"
      NALF, 5-6 (Winter), 140-149.
          Hughes uses three common themes of Blues: its love, bad
      luck, and idea of moving. One can no more separate the
      Blues-maker from his song than a dancer from his dance.
      [Compare with Yeats's "Among School Children."]

19   YESTADT, S. MARIE. "True American Poets: Their Influence on
      the Contemporary Art-Song," XUS, 10 (Spring), iii, 33-43.
          Langston Hughes and Walt Whitman left sound accounts of
      the way that things were in their social environment.
      Hughes's poetry, however, has more ideas. In the pierrot,
      one of his most interesting images, Hughes visualized him-
      self. Often songs are set to the pierrot poems.

1972 A BOOKS

1   DICKINSON, DONALD C. Bio-Bibliography of Langston Hughes.
      Hamden: Archon Books.
          Basically this is the same as the book copyrighted in
      1964 and abridged in DA of 1965. Here, however, Dickinson
      updates secondary entries to 1969. See 1964.A1; 1965.B1.

1972 B SHORTER WRITINGS

1   BREAUX, ELVRYN ELLISON. "Comic Elements in Selected Prose
      Works by James Baldwin, Ralph Ellison, and Langston Hughes,"
      DA (Oklahoma State University), 33 (July), 747 A.
          The authors use many comic elements [undefined] as well
      as a comic structure [undefined].

*2   BROWN, MICHAEL ROBERT. "Five Afro-American Poets: a History
      of the Major Poets and Their Poetry in the Harlem Renais-
      sance," DA (University of Michigan), 32 (January), 3990A.
          The historical and biographical context help to illumi-
      nate Hughes's work up to 1930.

1972

*3   BRYANT, JAMES DAVID. "Satire in the Work of Langston Hughes,"
      DA (Texas Christian University), 33 (September), 2362A.
         Cited in DA. A tone of attack modifies Hughes's
      humor, ridicule, irony, and social criticism (Chapter I).
      Hughes balances his attack against the American Dream as a
      satiric norm. Harlem is the satiric scene (Chapter III);
      Jim Crow, the final focus of criticism (Chapter IV).

4   BUSH, ROLAND C. "Négritude: A Sense of Reality," BlackW
      22 (November), 36-47.
         Like the works of Léopold Senghor and those of Aimé
      Césaire, Hughes presents the word-sorcerer who can confront
      European archetypes and destroy them.

5   BUTCHER, MARGARET JUST. "Formal Negro Poetry," in The Negro
      in American Culture. New York: Alfred A. Knopf, pp. 175-
      176.
         Since Hughes and Countee Cullen were the outstanding
      poets of the Negro Renaissance, one usually pairs them.
      Hughes, however, was experimental while Cullen was tradi-
      tional. Hughes's "Song to a Negro Wash Woman" and "Mother
      to Son" are "unsurpassed genre pictures of Negro women,"
      mothers whose fortitude is typical of "countless Negro moth-
      ers responsible for second and third generation progress."
      Today we compare Hughes to Sterling Brown rather than
      Countee Cullen, since Hughes and Brown were both concerned
      with the "revaluation of the Negro folk." Hughes's char-
      acterization of these people deviates from the norm. Never
      whining and never complaining, they are stoic, ironic, and
      often pessimistic. But they are never self-deluded.

6   _____. "The Negro in Modern American Fiction," in The Negro
      in American Culture. New York: Alfred A. Knopf.
         Not Without Laughter is more fine and realistic than
      most of its contemporaries.

7   FARRISON, W. EDWARD. "Langston Hughes: Poet of the Negro
      Renaissance," CLAJ, 15, No. 4 (June), 401-410.
         Hughes kept the original and noblest ideals of the Negro
      Renaissance: pride in heritage, temperance of race, and
      integration into the American mainstream. The title poem
      of The Weary Blues is some of the best Blues verse that
      Hughes ever wrote.

*8   HANSELL, WILLIAM HAROLD. "Positive Themes in the Poetry of
      Four Negroes," DA (University of Wisconsin, Madison), 33,
      (July), 754A.

Cited in DA. Hughes wanted to imitate Negro music in
his poetry because he thought that this music had universal
appeal.

9   JOANS, TED. "The Langston Hughes I Knew," BlackW, 21
     (September), 14-18.
          Hughes helped and encouraged me during my career. Long
     before many of the so-called hip Black poets, he was hip:
     "He told it like it is when it was not popular to do so."

10   RANDALL, DUDLEY. "The Black Aesthetic in the Thirties, For-
     ties, and Fifties," in The Black Aesthetic. Edited by
     Addison Gayle, Jr. New York: Anchor Books, pp. 212-221.
          Hughes's concerns changed from the glamor of night clubs
     to world-wide democracy and freedom. The writer ironically
     juxtaposes instances of injustice and the American Dream.

11   TAYLOR, PATRICIA E. "Langston Hughes and the Harlem Renais-
     sance, 1921-1931: Major Events and Publications," in
     Harlem Renaissance Remembered. Edited by Arna Bontemps.
     New York: Dodd, Mead, pp. 90-99.
          Hughes's productivity parallels other events such as
     the Garvey movement and the beginning and decline of the
     NAACP. The writer met important people: W. E. B. Du Bois,
     Mary McLeod Bethune, Walter White, Duke Ellington,
     Bojangles, Bessie Smith, Ethel Waters, Paul Robeson,
     V. C. Handy, and Richard Harrison. During the period
     A'Lelia Walker was a renowned giver of parties. Critics
     condemned Hughes's Fine Clothes to the Jew, but Not Without
     Laughter later outsold two earlier books. The poet admired
     Thurman, if anyone, but with ambivalence. Hughes was prob-
     ably not sexually active with his patron, since he was in-
     volved with "much younger women in Harlem."

1973 A BOOKS - NONE

1973 B SHORTER WRITINGS

1   ANON. "Langston Hughes Manuscripts," Ban, 56, 6-7.
          These complement the important group of 179 letters that
     Hughes wrote to Noel Sullivan, the famous art patron, be-
     tween 1932 and 1956. The collection contains various
     materials purchased from Roy Blackburn of Oakland, Hughes's
     secretary for a time: manuscripts, correspondence, in-
     scribed editions, photographs, and lecture programs. Here
     one finds "Mother to Child" with an attached note that any
     non-profit organization could use the play without fee. In

1973

the short stories, "The Professor" and "The Negro in the
Drawing Room," Hughes quietly captured the Black experience
of his time.

2   EMANUEL, JAMES A. "Christ in Alabama: Religion in the Poetry
    of Langston Hughes," in <u>Modern Black Poets</u>. Edited by
    Donald B. Gibson. Englewood Cliffs: Prentice Hall,
    pp. 57-68.
        Hughes's poetry suggests that religion "has been espe-
    cially valuable to Blacks." Two of his best and early
    poems, "Brass Spitoons" (1926) and "Negro Mother" (1931),
    celebrate the racial endurance that religious faith en-
    courages. To link Blacks with Christ, Hughes most often
    relies on the Holy Crucifixion as a metaphor. "Christ in
    Alabama" (1931) is a notable example. Hughes's ultimate
    point is that one's religion is one's prerogative.

3   HILL, ROY L. "The Significant Influence of Langston Hughes
    on the Thinking and the Inner Lives of Nine Contemporary
    Black Poets," <u>DA</u> (Rutgers University), 33 (March), 5124A.
        Cited in <u>DA</u>. The influence is on Imamu Amiri Baraka
    (LeRoi Jones), Gwendolyn Brooks, Mari Evans, Nikki Giovanni,
    Roy L. Hill, Jewel C. Lattimore, Don L. Lee, Carolyn M.
    Rodgers, and Sonia Sanchez. All believe in their works
    and themselves. Their verses reveal them to be guides in
    the Black community.

4   JEMIE, ONWUCHEKWA. "Dream Deferred: A Comment on Langston
    Hughes's Poetry," <u>DA</u> (Columbia University), 34 (July),
    p. 319A.
        Hughes is an innovator of the first rank and a "seminal
    figure in Afro-American literature." His article, "The
    Negro Artist and the Racial Mountain" (<u>The Nation</u>, 1926),
    began the principles of what has come to be a Black Esthetic.
    Hughes prefigured cultural nationalists such as Imamu Baraka
    (LeRoi Jones), Don Lee, Sonia Sanchez, Nikki Giovanni, and
    Askia Muhammed Touré. More completely than any other writer,
    Hughes captured the Blues as a cultural form of art. He
    dramatizes the tension between American "rhetoric and
    American reality."

5   KLOTMAN, PHYLLIS R. "Jesse B. Semple and the Narrative Art of
    Langston Hughes," <u>JNT</u>, 3 (January), 66-75.
        The narrative technique makes for the popularity of the
    tales: (1) the sure-fire appeal of the skit technique,
    (2) an apparent artlessness and simplicity in the develop-
    ment of theme and character, (3) reader identification, and
    (4) the intermittent sound of the Blues in prose. As a

straight man, Hughes's persona Boyd is the foil to Simple's
wit; his educated language is juxtaposed to Simple's Black
English which is rich in the folk idioms of Harlem.
Hughes's works reflect racial and human endurance.

6   PRESLEY, JAMES. "The Birth of Jesse B. Semple," SWR, 58
    (Summer), 219-225.
        Simple began in Hughes's weekly column and on the edi-
    torial page of the Chicago Defender. His birthday was
    February 13, 1943. Until Hughes's death in 1967, the
    character remained active and vocal.

7   SCARNHOST, GARY F. "Theme for English B," Explicator, 32
    (December), item 27.
        For all second-class citizens, this essay presents a
    theme of the universal life that prevails.

8   WAGNER, JEAN. "Langston Hughes," in Black Poets of the United
    States. Urbana: University of Illinois Press, pp. 385-474.
    Original edition in French: Les Poètes Nègres des États
    Unis, copyrighted 1962 by Librarie Istra, Paris.
        During the Harlem Renaissance, Hughes was highly original
    and most productive. He transformed the atavistic rhythms
    of American Blacks into moments of racial significance. He
    had weaknesses: excessiveness; occasionally unrestrained
    impulsiveness; frequent and unnecessary vulgarity; and cul-
    tivation of originality at any price. Hughes's achievement
    remains, nevertheless, as the freshest and most personal of
    the period. Montage of a Dream Deferred contains Hughes's
    boldest experiment with jazz techniques. In Ask Your Mama
    the understanding lies not in the relationship between
    image and reality (for this is unintelligible), but in the
    "kindred sonority and structure." Hughes voiced the
    "eternal aspirations of all men whose love is freedom."

9   WHITLOW, ROGER. Black American Literature. Chicago: Nelson
    Hall, p. 87.
        Not Without Laughter is a mediocre and partly autobio-
    graphical work about a young boy's early years in a segre-
    gated Kansas town.

10 YOUNG, JAMES O. Black Writers of the Thirties. Baton Rouge:
    Louisiana State University Press, p. 216.
        Hughes's work differed from other literature in the
    thirties by failing to show the romantic influence of the
    Renaissance. In Not Without Laughter, he criticizes the
    degeneration that white education causes in the life of
    Blacks. Although the narrative centers around Sandy,

1974

Hughes develops Aunt Hager most completely. To her he
attributes heroic stature, endurance, and appreciation for
beauty and laughter. Not Without Laughter was one of the
first novels by a black to examine the life of the common
folk on its own terms. The theme of The Ways of White Folks
is that whites attempt to shape blacks into preconceived
molds.

1974 A BOOKS

1 WALKER, ALICE. Langston Hughes, American Poet. New York:
Thomas Y. Crowell, 53 pp.
Biography for children. Hughes could not live with his
mother, who often moved to look for work. At Central High
in Cleveland, he wrote poems for the school magazine. He
dreamed of writing stories about Negroes that people would
read even after his death. In a quest for a summer job, he
discovered discrimination while still a young man. His
father thought that Black people, being poor, had no right
to laugh. Some Africans said that Langston Hughes looked
like a white man, but he always wrote truthfully about
Blacks. Their ability to laugh when feeling blue, he
thought, made them special. Upon his death in 1967 he
left to his friends the eternal knowledge of how to love
one another.

1974 B SHORTER WRITINGS

1 BROWN, LLOYD W. "The Portrait of the Artist as a Black American in the Poetry of Langston Hughes," SBL, 5 (Winter),
24-27.
Hughes's statement in "The Negro Artist and the Racial
Mountain" illuminates the symbolic role of the artist as
archetype. This archetype concerns the singer of the blues
as well as the dancer-poet or musician in general. More
than structure, art form is an expression of the writer's
ethnic and social experience. The nature of Hughes's
thematic choices remains constant.

2 DAVIS, ARTHUR P. "Langston Hughes," in From the Dark Tower.
Washington: Howard University Press, pp. 61-72.
Hughes was the most experimental and versatile author of
the Renaissance, and time may find him the greatest. "I
Too Sing America" was part of his credo. By example, he
showed the importance of the folk contribution to black
writing: blues, spirituals, ballads, jazz, and folk-speech.
Amid younger and more militant black writers, Hughes

preserved a much-needed sense of "tolerance and old-fashioned humor." Simplicity characterized all of his poetry. He used lynching to symbolize American injustice. Like other young Blacks of the thirties and forties, he saw hope for the oppressed in the Marxist position. Nothing, however, could disturb his "coolness," his ability to see two sides of any issue. Through the years, Hughes's treatment of African Négritude deepened and changed. The early poems strike a literary pose, but the later verses portray a real and embittered Africa. Hughes greatly influenced West African and West Indian Négritude. His greatest gift was laughter, and he had faith in the man in the streets.

3   JACKSON, BLYDEN and LOUIS D. RUBIN, JR. Black Poetry in America. Baton Rouge: Louisiana State University Press, pp. 51-53.
    With Countee Cullen and Claude McKay, Hughes is the third of the "three bright stars in the poetic firmament of the Renaissance"; he differed, however, in temperament. Hughes could dramatize the Negro experience of the American South as McKay and Cullen never could. In temperament, he, like Cullen, could have linked himself with Keats. Hughes does not stand between his reader and his folk portraits. Limited in range, his poetry does not grow. He liked experimentation, and his The Weary Blues "pioneered in the Renaissance." Jazz haunts all of his early verses. This writer was a great impressionist. He was not a genius at synthesizing "big things." In the thirties, he produced little in value, as compared with the forties and fifties.

4   ROSENBLATT, ROGER. "Not Without Laughter," in Black Fiction. Cambridge: Harvard University Press, pp. 76-84.
    Hughes implies some questions: Are academic and worldly educations equally valuable to a Black child? Is either valuable alone? Three forces influence Sandy before his schooling begins: Christianity, music, and laughter. To Hager, the Bible and the switch represent her faith. Sandy chooses Harriet as an ideal because she is honest with herself. When white protagonists in English literature move from innocence to experience, they can choose whether to remain innocent. But in Black American fiction no distinction exists between innocence and ignorance. Neither has any social benefit.

1975 A BOOKS

1   MANDELIK, PETER and STANLEY SCHATT. Concordance to Langston Hughes. Detroit: Gale Research Company, 295 pp.

1975

This book contains the following: identification code
used; abbreviations of poetry volumes and index to poem
titles; concordance to Hughes's poetry; numerical keywords
and colloquial contractions; statistical summary: word
frequencies in rank and order and words omitted from the
concordance. In revisions Hughes eliminated the Dunbar-
like dialect of The Weary Blues and Fine Clothes to the Jew.
Selected Poems and The Panther and the Lash show deletion
of political references to the thirties. See 1975.B5.

1975 B SHORTER WRITINGS

1   COBB, MARTHA K. "The Black Experience in the Poetry of
     Nicolás Guillén, Jacques Roumain, Langston Hughes,"
     DA (Catholic University of America), 35 (February),
     5392A-5393A.
         These three Black poets of the Americas represent dif-
     ferent cultural traditions--the Spanish, French, and North
     American. All matured in the first half of the Twentieth
     Century, a time of increased Black cultural awareness.
     Despite linguistic and national differences, these writers
     share common attitudes: confrontation (blackness in a
     hostile society); dualism (dilemma of both Black and Amer-
     ican); identity (search for one's humanity and one's heri-
     tage); and liberation (the struggle for freedom). Each
     writer moves from "early poetry that lyrically expresses
     indignation against injustices suffered by Black people
     to a poetic vision of human liberation for all oppressed
     peoples." The three also resemble each other in their
     usage of monologue and dialogue as well as in the blended
     cadence of language and music. Considered together, these
     writers indicate a need for "critically defining the char-
     acter and the attributes of a Black aesthetic in the
     Americas."

2   KLOTMAN, PHYLLIS R. "Langston Hughes's Jesse B. Semple and
     the Blues," Phylon, 36 (Fall), 68-77.
         The popularity of the tale depends on the artist's narra-
     tive technique: the appeal of the skit, the simplicity in
     developing theme and character, reader identification, and
     the intermittent sound of Blues prose. Throughout his works
     Hughes celebrates the "Afro-American ability to endure."
     Compare 1973.B5.

3   LOWERY, DELITTA MARTIN. "Selected Poems of Nicolás Guillén
     and Langston Hughes: Their Use of Afro-Western Folk Music
     Genres," DA (Ohio State University), 36 (September),
     1487A-1488A.

Guillén and Hughes translate folk music forms of African
oral tradition into the written genres of Western (European-
oriented) literature. Guillén uses the rhythmic complexity
and antiphonal structure of the <u>rumba</u> and the <u>son</u>; Hughes
employs the rhythms and the structure of call-response in
a folk language associated with blues and jazz. Chapters
are: (1) Defining folklore; (2) Origin of African-derived
oral traditions in New World; (3) Manifestations of African-
derived oral traditions in Cuba; (4-6) Guillén's imitation
of <u>rumba</u> and <u>son</u> in <u>Motives de son</u> (1930), <u>Sóngoro Cosongo</u>
(1931), and <u>West Indies LTD</u> (1934); (7) Manifestations of
African-derived oral traditions in U.S.; (7-10) Poems
illustrating Hughes's imitation of blues and jazz in <u>The</u>
<u>Weary Blues</u>, <u>Fine Clothes to the Jew</u>, and <u>Montage of a</u>
<u>Dream Deferred</u>--tracing the folk forms from 1920's up;
(11) summary contrasting the poets' styles.

4   MILLER, R. BAXTER. "'No Crystal Stair': Unity, Archetype,
    and Symbol in Langston Hughes's Poems on Women," <u>NALF</u>, 9
    No. 4 (Winter), 109-114.
        Comic, tragic, or heroic transformations of a traditional
    archetype give thematic unity to Hughes's poems on women.
    The quantity and range of his work generally distinguish
    it. By empathizing with a Christian woman, Hughes demon-
    strates his talent for creating an autonomous persona. His
    most personal poems, however, indicate humanism, as opposed
    to Christianity. "Mother to Son" and "Negro Mother" differ
    in form but are similar in their unity of vision and theme
    of endurance. Reprinted 1976.B4.

5   SCHATT, STANLEY. "Langston Hughes: The Minstrel as Artificer,"
    <u>JML</u>, 4, 115-120.
        Since many of Hughes's books are rare, few people recog-
    nize his numerous revisions. These vary, however, from
    minor changes in punctuation to additions of whole stanzas
    that indicate a shift in philosophical stance. Of 186
    verses in <u>Selected Poems</u>, fifty-nine were edited from
    earlier versions. Often changes consist of eliminating
    commas that precede dashes that remove Dunbar-like dialect.
    Revisions occasionally indicate the omission of outdated
    lines.

6   WINZ, CARY D. "Langston Hughes: A Kansas Poet in the Harlem
    Renaissance," <u>KanQ</u>, 7 (Summer), 58-69.
        The most brilliant of the Harlem Renaissance poets,
    Hughes created "lively portraits of Negro Urban Experience."
    His grandmother, Mary Simpson Langston, greatly influenced
    his early years, and in his poetry Africa became a symbol

1976

of "lost roots, of a distant past that could never be re-
trieved." Except for this early verse, however, he devoted
less attention to this subject than did other Renaissance
poets. The power of "Christ in Alabama," a verse, came
characteristically from "using inflammatory images to pro-
duce a cool, controlled anger." Most interesting was
Hughes's innovative style--his experimentations with blues
and jazz and other folk forms. The verse "Song for a Dark
Girl" shows grief and moral outrage, but the volume
Montage of a Dream Deferred fully represents Harlem life.
     In Not Without Laughter, Hager is more fully developed
than Tempy and Harriett. By her sense of morality and
responsibility, this last woman influences the protagonist,
her grandson. On the contrary, Sandy's father, Jimboy,
symbolizes nature and vitality. Sandy is never fully developed, and the most interesting portraits remain periph-
eral. But even if the plot is weak, the characters are
believable. More important, Hughes gives an unsurpassed
description of small town Negro life. His acquaintance
with poverty was much more accurate than that of other
Renaissance writers who glamorized poor peoples' lives.
During the depression, Hughes moved closer to communism.
His poetry became more angry and propagandistic; his political activity unfortunately undermined the quality of his
verse. While Hughes does not often return to his small
town roots, he "maintained a commitment to racial pride
and a belief in the dignity of the common man--values he
had acquired from his grandmother in Kansas."

1976 A BOOKS

  1 JEMIE, ONWUCHEKWA. Langston Hughes: An Introduction to the
       Poetry. New York: Columbia University Press, 234 pp.
          One should evaluate Hughes from a dual perspective of
       folk tradition as well as struggle and protest. Chapters
       include "Hughes's Black Aesthetic"; "Shadow of the Blues";
       "Jazz, Jive and Jam"; "Or Does It Explode?"; "The Dream
       Keeper"; "Hughes and the Evolution of Consciousness in Black
       Poetry." Peripheral matter consists of chronological sketch,
       notes, bibliography, and index. By his themes, recreated from
       Black folk culture, Hughes prefigures the cultural national-
       ism of the 1960's and 1970's--Hoyt Fuller, Ron Karenga, and
       Amiri Baraka--all evolving from Richard Wright. For Hughes,
       jazz represents life. If this jazz, however, is instrumental
       and aggressive, Blues is vocal and mellow. Of Hughes's
       first five books, only Fine Clothes to the Jew and The
       Negro Mother are entirely social or "modeled on Black folk

forms." The "I" in Hughes is the collective character of
race, insider; "me," on the contrary, is the detached self,
outsider. Hughes recognizes the chasm that exists between
"formal complexity" and "literary worth." His sensibility
took root in two radical decades, the thirties and the sixties. For him the central types were Boyd and Semple,
Sancho Panza and Don Quioxte. Hughes portrays the realist
and the dreamer.

1976 B SHORTER WRITINGS

1   BERRY, FAITH. "Did Van Vechten Make or Take Hughes' Blues?"
    BlackW (February), pp. 22-28.
        Van Vechten's only influence on The Weary Blues was that
    of a literary agent. The white novelist and critic frowned
    upon Hughes's poems of social protest from 1925 onward.
    During the 1930's and even afterwards, he discouraged them.
    Although Hughes wrote a Blues song for Nigger Heaven, he
    never confessed it. Despite being humorous and jovial, he
    had an uncanny sense of the white exploitation of Blacks.
    If he ever equated Van Vechten with such a practice, no
    explicit admission ever occurred.

2   MILLER, R. BAXTER. "'Done Made Us Leave Our Home': Langston
    Hughes's Not Without Laughter--Unifying Image and Three
    Dimensions," Phylon, 37, No. 4 (Winter), 362-369.
        The image of home unifies Not Without Laughter. Hughes
    works within a long tradition ranging from Homer to Baraka
    (Jones) in verse and from Charles Dickens to James Baldwin
    in prose. This image has meaning on three levels: the
    mythical, the historical, and the social. Plot does not
    exist in the traditional sense because "character reveals
    action instead of the other way around." From an initial
    situation of home, the reader moves first to a disintegra-
    tion of the Williams family and then to a process of this
    family's recreation.

3   _____. "'A Mere Poem': 'Daybreak in Alabama,' a Resolution
    to Langston Hughes's Theme of Music and Art," Obsidian, 2,
    No. 2 (Summer), 30-37. First presented as a paper at CLA
    Convention in New Orleans in April, 1975.
        "Daybreak" is Hughes's final and most aesthetic defini-
    tion of music and art. It casts a backward light on his
    best renditions of this theme in poetry, fiction, and essay.
    The structure of the poem makes the theme organic. In the
    poetry, Hughes transforms the theme in three ways: art as
    an emblem of the future; celebrating the dead or the dying,
    the folk heroic; suggesting the motifs of freedom and quest.

1976

> Chronologically, "Daybreak" is on the border line (1940)
> between Hughes's "treatment of art as praise and his depic-
> tion of art as celebration." By apocalyptic harmony, "Day-
> break" resolves the different strands of Hughes's short
> fiction--contemplation, orphic power, and anticipation of
> Messianic presence. "Daybreak" resolves the inconsistency
> of Hughes's social essays.

4 _____. "'No Crystal Stair': Unity, Archetype, and Symbol in
Langston Hughes's Poems on Women," in <u>Writing About Black
Literature</u>. Edited by Chester J. Fontenot. Lincoln:
Nebraska Curriculum Development Center, pp. 147-159.
See 1975.B4 for annotation.

5 _____. "'Some High Ol' Lonesome Hill': The Different Trans-
cendences of Langston Hughes and Sterling Brown," <u>MR</u>
(Scheduled Fall, but delayed, expected Winter or Spring,
1978).
Hughes and Brown are poets who go different ways down
the same road of folk materials. Hughes is a romantic
visionary; Brown, a dramatic realist. The two authors have
diverse ways of portraying literary character and contrasting settings of geography. Their forms and usages of music
differ and they have opposite conceptions of Nature and the
universe. Hughes reaches the universal by allegory, col-
lectivity, and symbol; Brown, by the careful juxtaposition
of characters who are foils.

6 WILLIAMS, MELVIN G. "Langston Hughes's Jesse B. Semple: A
Black Walter Mitty," <u>NALF</u>, 10, No. 2 (Summer, 1976), 66-69.
Semple is such a dreamer that one can call him a Black
Walter Mitty. The original creator of the type was James
Thurber. Hughes's character, like Thurber's, is a small
man in a "world of aggressive women." Semple, however,
experiences the poor and Black conditions that did not
affect Mitty. Occasionally, Semple has either petty vin-
dictiveness or self-pity. Sometimes he dreams about dream-
ing. If his fantasies do not concern getting even, they
deal with the process of ego building.

1977 A BOOKS - NONE

1977 B SHORTER WRITINGS

1 MILLER, R. BAXTER. "'Even After I Was Dead': 'The Big Sea'--
Paradox, Preservation, and Holistic Time," <u>BALF</u>, 11
(Summer), 39-45.

In a difficult or disorganized structure, fusing time, The Big Sea interweaves the themes of paradox and eternality. Like George Walker and Bert Williams, the Hughes in the narrative is immortal, for the book freezes characters outside of time. The work creates a detached self that belongs in successful fiction, but not an engaged self that belongs in great autobiography. More than the real Hughes, the imagined Hughes is naive. The latter's break with his patron and his quarrel with Hurston over Mule Bone lack subjectivity. The Big Sea, however, preserves the values that inform Hughes's literary world: the wisdom of old folk, the sacredness of life, and the indignation at the exploitation of Black art.

2   VIDAL, DAVID. "What Happens to a Dream: This One Lives," New York Times (March 24), p. B-1.
        Not far from Hughes's former Harlem home, eight black writers, poets, and teachers gathered at the City College of New York yesterday. There they celebrated Hughes's seventy-fifth birthday. About five hundred listeners, mostly students, concluded that Hughes's dream will endure. Professional participants were as follows: John Henrik Clark, teacher of Black studies at CCNY and a friend of the poet during forty of Hughes's forty-three years in New York City; June Jordan who said she considered herself a "daughter" of Mr. Hughes; Paule Marshall, another writer and friend who traveled with him twelve years ago in Europe; Professor Addison Gayle, Jr. of the Bernard M. Baruch College; Wilfred Carty, another city college professor and moderator of the symposium; Nathan I. Huggins of Columbia; Quincy Troupe of Richmond College; John A. Davis, city college political scientist.

3   WILLIAMS, MELVIN G. "The Gospel According to Simple," BALF 11 (Summer), 46-48.
        Because Jesse B. Semple is a Black Everyman, investigating the use of the Bible and the church in the five Simple books is a worthwhile contribution to Black Studies. Occasionally Semple prays. Because his youth saturated him with Christianity and the Bible, he now draws upon them almost automatically. The story of Adam and Eve is one of his favorites.

Gwendolyn Brooks

Major Writings by Gwendolyn Brooks

A Street in Bronzeville, 1945

Annie Allen, 1949

Maud Martha, 1953

Bronzeville Boys and Girls, 1956

The Bean Eaters, 1960

Selected Poems, 1963

In the Mecca, 1968

Riot, 1970

Aloneness, 1971

A Broadside Treasury, 1971

Family Pictures, 1971

Jump Bad, 1971

The World of Gwendolyn Brooks, 1971

Report from Part One, 1972

The Tiger Who Wore White Gloves, 1974

Beckonings, 1975

Writings about
Gwendolyn Brooks, 1944-1977

1944 A BOOKS - NONE

1944 B SHORTER WRITINGS

1   ANON. "Prizes," <u>CDN</u> (August 3).
        Brooks, a resident of E. 63rd Street, won the Eunice
Tientjens award of $25 for the best short poems submitted
in a poetry workshop.

2   ANON. "Note to 'Negro Hero,'" <u>Common Ground</u>, 5, p. 45.
        Dorie Miller, the hero of Brooks's poem is a young mess
attendant who won the Navy Cross at Pearl Harbor. Devoted
to duty, he displayed extraordinary courage and disregard
for his own personal safety during the attack. After members of the gun crew had been killed or wounded, Miller
manned a machine gun on the S. S. Arizona and shot down
four Japanese planes. While enemy bullets whistled, he
carried his wounded captain to safety. Since December 1943,
he has been missing in the Southwest Pacific.

1945 A BOOKS - NONE

1945 B SHORTER WRITINGS

1   ANON. Review of <u>A Street in Bronzeville</u>, <u>KiR</u> (July 15),
       p. 306.
        Brooks is gifted, passionate, and authentic. Although
the themes are not original, the feeling is fresh. The
melody and versification are individual. Wrought into the
texture of the poem, the imagery is arresting.

2   ANON. Review of <u>A Street in Bronzeville</u>, <u>New Yorker</u>, 21
       (September 22), 80.
        With traditional forms, Brooks mixes the vigorous folk
poetry of her people. She writes with a style, sincerity,
and minimum of sentimentality. Her folk poetry of the
city is particularly fresh.

1945

3   ANON. Review of A Street in Bronzeville, WLJ (October), p. 99.
         The work is vivid, individualistic in style and forceful
         in effect.

4   ANON. "'Women of the Year' List Names Two Chicagoans," CS
         (December 28), Sect. 2, p. 21.
             One is Brooks, 28, author of A Street in Bronzeville.
         Betsy Talbot Blackwell, editor-in-chief of Mademoiselle,
         announced the awards yesterday.

5   ANON. "Songs and Funeral Chants," CDN (August 22).
             A Street in Bronzeville ranges from blues ballads and
         funeral chants to verse in high humor. With both clarity
         and insight, it mirrors the impressions of life in an urban
         Negro community. The best poem is "The Sundays of Satin-
         Legs Smith," a poignant and hour-by-hour page out of a
         zoot-suiter's life. A subtle change of pace proves
         Brooks's facility in a variety of poetic forms.

6   HUMPHRIES, ROLPHE. "Bronzeville," NYTBR (November 4), p. 14.
             In A Street in Bronzeville we have a "good book and real
         poet." If the idiom is colloquial, the language is uni-
         versal. Brooks commands both the colloquial and more aus-
         tere rhythms. She can vary manner and tone. In form, she
         demonstrates a wide range: quatrains, free verse, ballads,
         and sonnets--all appropriately controlled. The longer line
         suits her better than the short, but she is not verbose.
         In some of the sonnets she uses an abruptness of address
         that is highly individual.

*7   SAVER, C. M. Springfield Republican (September 30), p. 42.
             Unlocatable. Listed in Loff (1973.B6). No title given.

8   WILDER, AMOS R. "Sketches from Life," Poetry, 67-68
         (December), 164-166.
             Review of A Street in Bronzeville. Brooks shows a
         capacity to combine race with the best attainments of con-
         temporary poetry. Two sections, including the title one,
         are unexciting vignettes of sentiment and character. The
         pieces have the spice and movement found in the better
         Negro poets. "The Sundays of Satin-Legs Smith" evokes the
         Negro's urge for "splendor, ceremony, and gusto." In the
         sonnet series "Gay Chaps at the Bar," sophistication of
         craft and theme add to the "volatility of the author's
         talent." A reading of the modern poets underlies the com-
         petence of her work. Although some of the verse is unex-
         citing, one finds much promise and resource for future work.

<u>1946 A BOOKS - NONE</u>

<u>1946 B SHORTER WRITINGS</u>

1   ANON. "Chicago Poet Wins $1,000 Arts Prize," <u>CS</u> (May 6).
          As a Chicagoan and former Chicagoan--respectively--
     Gwendolyn Brooks and Peter DeVries received grants of
     $1,000 each from the American Academy of Arts and Letters
     and the National Institute of Arts and Letters at a dinner
     in New York on May 17. Brooks is a 29-year-old Kansas-born
     poet and contributor to <u>Poetry</u>; DeVries is a former co-
     editor of <u>Poetry</u>, but now is on the staff of the <u>New Yorker</u>.

2   ANON. "S-Side Center to Honor Author," <u>CDN</u> (June 13).
          A tea will honor Brooks at 3 p.m. Sunday in Corpus
     Christi Center, 4622 Parkway.

3   ANON. "The Sun Salutes Gwendolyn Brooks," <u>CS</u> (January 1),
     p. 12.
          Today the Chicago Sun salutes Gwendolyn Brooks, a
     Chicago poet who was chosen one of <u>Mademoiselle</u> magazine's
     "Women of the Year." From Betsy Talbot Blackwell, editor-
     in-chief of the magazine, Brooks received a medal for <u>A</u>
     <u>Street in Bronzeville</u>.

*4   EDWARDS, THYRA. "She'll Write Novel of Normal Negro Family,"
     <u>Now</u> (July).
          Unlocatable. Listed in Loff (1973.B6).

5   NELSON, STARR. "Social Comment in Poetry," <u>SatR</u>, 29
     (January-June), 15.
          Review of <u>A Street in Bronzeville</u>. The volume is "both
     a work of art and a poignant social document." The sonnets
     are not poor. After the abandon, pungency, and clarity of
     the ballads or genre pieces, however, they seem strained
     and contrived.

<u>1947 A BOOKS - NONE</u>

<u>1947 B SHORTER WRITINGS</u>

1   ANON. "Guggenheim Fellowships Won by 4 Educators, Authors
     Here," <u>CS</u> (April 14).
          This is Brooks's second award from the foundation.
     Other recipients are as follows: Dr. Robert LeRoy
     Platzmen, chemist for study of nuclear radiations;
     Dr. Wallace Fowler, Associate Professor of Humanities,

1949

for his proposed study of the poetry of Stephen Mallarmé;
Dr. Paul Hene, Associate Professor of Philosophy, for in-
vestigating the theory of meaning; Dr. Paul Halmos, Assistant Professor of Mathematics, for mathematical theory.

1949 A BOOKS - NONE

1949 B SHORTER WRITINGS

1 ANON. "Autograph Party for Miss Brooks," CDN (August 31).
On September 18, friends of Brooks plan an autographing
party for her at International House on the University of
Chicago campus.

2 ANON. Review of Annie Allen, Booklist (November 1).
Annie Allen moves beyond A Street in Bronzeville:
"Again the themes are mainly those of city people, but here
the expression is more general and less identifiably Negro."

3 ANON. Review of Annie Allen, KiR (June 15), p. 319.
In some respects this volume does not match the high
standards of the first. Although having less technical
competence and precision, it is interesting and refreshing.
By having a "warm animal vitality," the work shows a quality often lacking in American poetry.

4 ANON. Review of Annie Allen, New Yorker 25 (December 17),
130.
Brooks has allowed herself much experimentation in
language, and not all of it succeeds. Her basic sense of
form, however, is still remarkable. She can make a sonnet
as "tight as a bowstring."

5 ANON. Review of Annie Allen, SFC (September 18), p. 18.
Annie Allen will widen Brooks's reputation. Having a
keen mind, she severely controls lyrical concreteness.
Gwendolyn Brooks can be compared only with Gwendolyn Brooks.
She is really remarkable.

6 B.[RADLEY], V.[AN] A.[LLEN]. "Miss Brooks' Sensitive and Sure
Verse," CDN (August 24), p. 32.
Among the newer poets, Brooks has shown exceptional
promise. A Street in Bronzeville won immediate acclaim,
and Annie Allen is a further measure of her talent. Her
imagery is keener; her technique, shrewd and sure. Having
an economy of phrase, she possesses an imagery that is
sharp, distinctive, and often startling. At times Brooks
comes perilously close to "yoking art to propaganda."

7   HUMPHRIES, ROLPHE. "Verse Chronicle," The Nation, 169
     (September 24), 306.
          Review of Annie Allen. Although this book resembles
     A Street in Bronzeville, it lacks the self-consciousness
     that occasionally "made one a little uncomfortable in read-
     ing her first book." Her weaknesses are awkwardness and
     naiveté when the big word or spectacular rhyme carries her
     away. The first two sections contain more of this than the
     third. Her strengths are boldness and invention. She should
     avoid her weaknesses but favor her strengths.

8   KENNEDY, LEE. "Chicago's Finest Writer," CST (August 29),
     p. 43.
          Brooks's second book establishes her as the "finest
     thing that has happened to Chicago writing since Nelson
     Algren." Like Hughes, Brooks is concerned with the "limited
     lives and circumscribed aspirations of poor Negro Americans."
     Being simply lyrical, Annie Allen is her best poetry. "Men
     of Careful Turns," the last poem, is a sober and magnificent
     speech against the racial inequality which is bondage with
     politeness.

9   LECHLINTER, RUTH. "Love Songs," NYHT (September 25), Sec. 7,
     p. 44.
          Brooks's individualized staccato manner--the partial
     statement, the deliberately broken scansion, the startling
     particularized image--give newness to the "traditional
     lyric or ballad form of the poems." "The Anniad" is a
     difficult verse because rhetoric mars a clarity of communi-
     cation. In a kind of cinematic drama, Brooks mixes sur-
     realism, bacchanalian images, religion and classical
     references. The sonnets that follow--which express a
     mother's concern for her children--have an emotion that
     is smoother and cleaner.

10   REDDING, J. SAUNDERS. "Cellini-like Lyrics," SatR, 32
     (September 17), 23, 27.
          In Annie Allen Brooks goes a long way toward realizing
     the poetic gifts manifest in A Street in Bronzeville. Her
     verses are as artistically sure, emotionally firm, and
     aesthetically complete as a silver figure by Cellini. Her
     talent finds expression with richness and warmth. Brooks
     should avoid the "obscure and the too oblique." Although
     her style seems naturally indirect, she is at her best
     when being direct.

1950 A BOOKS - NONE

1950

1950 B SHORTER WRITINGS

1   ANON. "Announcement: the 1949 Awards," <u>Poetry</u>, 75
     (October-March), 93-97.
        Brooks wins the Eunice Tientjens Award of $100 for a
     poem or group of poems by an American citizen published in
     <u>Poetry</u> during its thirty-seventh year. The prize was
     given for "Four Poems" in the March issue of 1949. Some
     previous winners were John Ciardi, 1944; Alfred Hayes,
     1946; Theodore Roethke, 1947; and Peter Viereck, 1948.

2   ANON. "Chi Poet Wins Pulitzer Prize," <u>NYAN</u> (May 6), pp. 1, 6.
        A quiet housewife and mother wins a $500 prize for
     <u>Annie Allen</u>. When questioned about Brooks's being the first
     Negro to win the award, a spokesman for Columbia said that
     no one kept records of race and that the university did not
     know Brooks's color until receiving a picture of her after
     having made the decision.

3   ANON. "Garlands from Morningside Heights," <u>SatR</u>, 33 (May 13),
     18.
        The Pulitzer judges have recognized a young Negro writer
     of remarkable talent. Most reviewers spoke of her work in
     terms of promise rather than of fulfillment.

4   ANON. "Guest at Tea," <u>CDN</u> (June 9).
        At a tea Tuesday evening, June 13, Brooks will be the
     guest of honor. The meeting will take place at the South
     Parkway YWCA.

5   ANON. "Gwendolyn Brooks to Be Honored," <u>CDN</u> (May 31), p. 34.
        At a tea from 4 to 6 p.m. in the club rooms of the Cliff
     Dwellers, 220 S. Michigan Avenue, the Society of Midland
     Authors will honor Brooks on Friday.

6   ANON. "Poetry," <u>CDN</u> (May 20), p. 3.
        Brooks will read from her work at 3:30 p.m., Wednesday,
     May 24, in the University of Chicago classics building,
     1000 E. 59th Street.

7   ANON. "The Pulitzer," <u>CDN</u> (May 2).
        The prize for the year's best book of poetry went to
     Brooks, a Chicago Negro.

8   ANON. "Pulitzer Poetess at Library Nov. 2," <u>CDN</u> (November 1),
     p. 34.
        Brooks will speak on "Reading and Writing Poetry" at
     12:15 p.m., Thursday, Nov. 5, in the Chicago Public Library.

During the noon-hour book talk, Brooks will read some of
her poetry and tell how she came to write it.

9   ANON. "Pulitzer Prize Announced by Columbia University,"
     PW, 157 (May), 1972.
         Brooks's Annie Allen won the $500 prize for a "distin-
     guished volume of verse."

10   ANON. Review of Annie Allen, USQB (March), p. 21.
         Like A Street in Bronzeville, this work explores the
     life of the Northern and urban ghetto, but here Brooks
     moves from her earlier realism to lyric emotion. Elabora-
     tion and experimentation in language have attracted her,
     since she wants to liberate herself from set patterns and
     to make her work variegated. The story of Annie Allen
     becomes a "kind of kaleidoscopic dream." Despite moments
     of extravagance, firmness and form hold the book together.

11   ANON. "S. Siders Honor Pulitzer Poet," CST (May 22).
         More than 200 Southside Leaders applaud Brooks's winning.
     Langston Hughes leads the reception at the Southside Com-
     munity Arts Center at 3831 Michigan Avenue. [Brooks tells
     me this never happened.]

12   ANON. "S. Side Wife Wins Pulitzer Poetry Award," CST (May 2).
         Brooks, A South-Side housewife, received the Pulitzer
     Prize for poetry. A resident of Wentworth, she is the
     first Negro woman so honored.

13   ANON. Who's Who in Chicago and Illinois, Chicago: A. A.
     Marquis Co.
         Brooks was born in Topeka, Kansas on June 7, 1917. Her
     parents were David Anderson and Keziah Corinne Brooks. The
     daughter graduated from Wilson Junior College in Chicago in
     1936. She was married to Henry L. Blakely on September 17,
     1939. She has a son, Henry L., III. In 1945 Mademoiselle
     magazine recognized her as one of the ten women of the year.
     She received awards from the American Academy of Arts and
     Letters in 1946 and 1947. [Please note that many books of
     this kind merely reprint the same information. When they
     do, I shall make a cross-reference to this entry.]

14   ANON. Who's Who in the Midwest, Vol. 9, Chicago: Marquis
     Who's Who.
         Brooks won the poetry award from the Friends of Litera-
     ture. She has been an instructor at Columbia College, a
     member of Society Midland Authors, and a reviewer for CST.
     See also 1950.B13.

1950

15   DEUTSCH, BABETTE. "Six Poets," Yale Review, 39 (Winter),
      362-363.
          This reviews Annie Allen and the following: Rosalie
      Moore, The Grasshopper's Man; Louis Simpson, The Arrivistes:
      Poems; José Garcia Valla, Volume Two; Sister Maury Jeremy,
      Dialogue with an Angel; and Theodore Spencer, An Acre in
      the Seed. To Brooks, Deutsch dedicates a paragraph--less
      space than he gives any other poet. Brooks uses conven-
      tional forms, but her tightly locking rhythms "constrict
      her unduly." She writes verses of statement that would be
      more effective as verses of understatement. Although she
      pulls her themes mainly from the world of the urban Negro,
      she fails to make the most of her material. The value of
      the work lies in the poet's prevailing attitude, for she
      mingles vitality and compassion. If this manner is not
      unique to Negroes, they demonstrate it with remarkable
      frequency.

16   DREER, HERMAN. "Gwendolyn Brooks," in American Literature by
      Negro Authors. New York: McMillan.
          Biographical information. See 1950.B13.

17   FLEMING, JAMES G. and CHRISTIAN E. BUREKE, eds. Who's Who in
      Colored America. New York: Christian E. Bureke and Asso-
      ciates, p. 57.
          Brooks's verse has appeared in Poetry, Common Ground,
      and Yale Review. Richard Wright, William Rose Benét,
      Carl Van Vechten, and others have acclaimed her. She won
      two Guggenheim fellowships, one for 1946 and another for
      1947. Four times she won the poetry workshop award given
      by the Midwestern Writers' Conference. Concerning religion,
      she is a Colored Methodist Episcopalian. See also 1950.B13.

18   HARRIOTT, FRANK. "The Life of a Pulitzer Poet," ND (August),
      pp. 14-16.
          Brooks says that winning the Pulitzer prize has not
      changed her attitude toward her writing. Some critics
      said that A Street in Bronzeville had humanity but no
      technical refinement; others, that Annie Allen had tech-
      nical refinement but no humanity. Now she tries to strike
      a balance.

19   HAZARD, ELOISE PERRY. "A Habit of Firsts," SatR (May 20),
      p. 23.
          Brooks remembers the numerous slips of rejection that
      preceded her first publication in American Childhood at 14.
      She remembers, too, her publication in Poetry at 28. Her
      early attempts at verse, she thinks, were very poor. She

92

learned much about technique in 1941 from Inez Boulton,
when Boulton directed a poetry class for Negroes at the
South-Side Community Center. Brooks admires Eliot's style
more than his content. She also admires Elinor Wylie's
style. Although Brooks's interest inclines toward modern
poets, she finds something of value in poets of all periods.

20 HUGHES, LANGSTON. "Name, Race, and Gift in Common," Voices,
    No. 140 (Winter), pp. 54-56.
        Brooks is a "very accomplished poet." Often condensing
    her lines to the sparest expression of the greatest meaning,
    she creates a "kind of word shorthand that defies immediate
    grasp." Although the poems of Annie Allen are less simple
    and direct than those in A Street in Bronzeville, they
    yield as much interest and emotional impact. If one reads
    carefully, Annie Allen shows first a progression from child-
    hood to an age of love and then a movement from love to
    motherhood. The third section, "The Womanhood," is most
    effective. Brooks's personae are alive, hopeful, and
    contemporary.

21 KUNITZ, STANLEY. "Bronze By Gold," Poetry, 76 (April 15),
    52-56.
        Brooks's work is always "warmly and generously human."
    More than her contemporaries, she stands free of anxiety
    and guilt. A modesty exists in her work. She uses her
    Negro and urban milieu naturally, but does not strain
    for shock or depth. She does not pretend to speak for a
    people. For her, the sonnet is home. The tightness of
    the form makes her disciplined and organizes her attitudes.
    She has as many kinds of "rightness" as any poet of her
    generation.

22 McGINLEY, PHYLLIS. "Poetry for Prose Readers," NYTBR,
    (January 22), p. 7.
        Review of Annie Allen. This book is talented and lyrical.
    It is uneven and as young and fresh as poetry itself. In
    verses such as "those little booths in Benvenutis," Brooks
    is a "clever if somewhat trite social critic." These and
    other pieces generally fail to match "The Anniad," which
    has much insight, wisdom, and pity. Technically dazzling,
    this little poem combines storytelling with lyric elegance.
    I hope that the unevenness of the work is the fault of
    youth and editors. Brooks creates unbearable excitement
    when she forgets her social conscience and her Guggenheim
    scholarship.

1950

23   PARKE, RICHARD H. "South Pacific Wins 1950 Pulitzer Prize,"
      NYT (May 2), p. 23.
           Brooks won the prize in poetry for Annie Allen. Her
      work has been described as a "small Spoon River Anthology
      of the Negro."

24   ROETHE, ANNA. Current Biography. New York: H. W. Wilson.
           See 1950.B13. Roethe quotes: 1945.B5; 1945.B7;
      1949.B9; 1950.B10, B19, B21, and B22.

1952 A BOOKS - NONE

1952 B SHORTER WRITINGS

1   ANON. "Chicago," CST (2 November).
          Harper's just accepted Brooks's first novel.

1953 A BOOKS - NONE

1953 B SHORTER WRITINGS

1   ANON. Review of Maud Martha, Booklist (October), p. 365.
          The novel moves from childhood to motherhood, and the
     prose has the "rhythmic beauty of free verse."

2   ANON. Review of Maud Martha, KiR (July 15), p. 458.
          Having much of the quality found in Brooks's poetry, the
     novel is a succession of fragile sequences that are
     suggestive.

3   ANON. Review of Maud Martha, New Yorker, 29 (October 10), 142.
          The work is not a novel but a "series of sketches." In
     style it is impressionistic, since the details pile up in
     order to create a single effect. This style is insuffi-
     ciently sharp or firm. It can neither "do justice to her
     remarkable gift for mimicry" nor equal her ability to con-
     vert unhappiness and joy into a joke.

4   ANON. Review of Maud Martha, WLJ (November-December), p. 259.
          Maud Martha wanted a good life and tried to make one.
     Despite disappointments, she succeeded.

5   BRADLEY, VAN ALLEN. "Negro's Life Here Effectively Portrayed
     in First Novel," CDN (September 30), p. 26.
          On Maud Martha. Brooks strikes at the "twisted roots of
     America's racial antagonisms." Maud Martha is magnificent,

and she exists within the narrow confines of 180 moving
pages. Through her we learn more than "any other contemporary novelist" has told about Negro life in Chicago.

6   BUTCHER, FANNY. "Swift, Sharp Prose by a Poet," CMBST
     (October 14), Sec. IV, p. 11.
         Maud Martha lacks the form of a novel. Within its
     universal femininity lies something vividly and intensely
     ethnic. This novel is more illuminating about racial
     relations than hundreds of books that discuss them.

7   KOGAN, HERMAN. "Two Chicagoans' Charm," CST (October 4),
     Sec. 2, p. 6.
         Because Brooks is a poet turned novelist, much of the
     "subdued charm" comes from her feeling for the beauty of
     words. Although she sketches her heroine--rather than
     drawing in deep detail--she has the "poetess' eye...the
     revealing phrase," shows some subdued inflections suggest-
     ing meanings far beyond the stated fact. With sharpness
     and economy, she reveals the city Negro. Brooks has
     effectively employed her artistry in this "touching and
     appealing little book."

8   _____. "Many Chicago Writers on Fall Publishing Lists," CST
     (July 12), Sec. 2, p. 6.
         Brooks's Maud Martha is one of only two novels by
     present Chicagoans and her first prose work.

9   MONJO, NICHOLAS. "Young Girl Growing Up," SatR, 36 (October),
     41.
         Review of Maud Martha. It is an "ingratiating first
     novel." The form is a random narration of incidents that
     are loosely assembled. The validity of Brooks's characters
     is beyond question. She brings the precision and vividness
     of the poet to them.

10   ROSENBERGER, COLEMAN. "A Work of Art and Jeweled Precision,"
     NYHTBR (October 18), p. 4.
         Review of Maud Martha. The same imprint of identity,
     which distinguished Brooks's two volumes of poetry, suf-
     fuses this volume of prose: sharp insight, warmth, joy of
     literary effect, and perfection of phrase or word. The
     word "novel" is imprecise because the work is a portrait
     and mosaic. The unity of the work is that of an unfolding
     life. Maud Martha is small but superb.

1954 A BOOKS - NONE

1954

1954 B SHORTER WRITINGS

1   OTTLEY, ROI. "Poet Finds Universe in Negro Life," <u>CST</u>
       (May 16), III, p. 3.
           By reading accurately and deeply into Negro experience,
       Brooks has accomplished the unusual and related poetry
       directly to life.

1955 A BOOKS - NONE

1955 B SHORTER WRITINGS

1   CROCKETT, JAQUELINE. "An Essay on Gwendolyn Brooks," <u>NHB</u>,
       19 (November), 37-39.
           <u>A Street in Bronzeville</u> is a "beautiful and poetic so-
       cial document." The richness, intensity, and warmth of
       <u>Annie Allen</u> make it valuable. Of all the verses, the final
       one, "men of careful turns," was most beautiful.

2   HERZBERG, MAX J., ed. <u>The Reader's Encyclopedia of American
       Literature</u>. New York: Thomas Y. Crowell.
           Brooks published her first poem in the then popular
       magazine, <u>American Childhood</u>. At 17, she became a frequent
       contributor of poetry to the <u>Chicago Defender</u>. In her books
       she has relied on personal experience and background to con-
       trast black and white races.

3   KUNITZ, STANLEY J. <u>Twentieth Century Authors</u>. New York:
       H. W. Wilson.
           <u>See</u> 1950.B13. Cites 1949.B7, and 1953.B10.

4   OTTLEY, ROI. "Woman Poet Probes Life of City's Negroes," <u>CT</u>
       (October 15), p. 17.
           Brooks has written excitingly of the people on the
       South-Side. Her tales are "simple stories about Negroes."
       Without allowances for sex or race, she wants her work to
       be judged for its worth.

1956 A BOOKS - NONE

1956 B SHORTER WRITINGS

1   ANON. Review of <u>Bronzeville Boys and Girls</u>, <u>KiR</u> (October 15),
       p. 788.
           These verses for children have the delicacy of mood and
       desire that characterize Gwendolyn Brooks's descriptions
       of the urban Negro.

2   ANON. Review of <u>Bronzeville Boys and Girls</u>, <u>NYHTBR</u>
     (November 18), p. 8.
          The reader senses that Brooks has experienced each
     child's joys, sorrows, and keen perceptions. These Bronze-
     ville boys and girls are universal.

3   ANON. "New Books for the Younger Reader's Library," <u>NYHTBR</u>
     (December).
          Only Ronni Solbert's pictures indicate that the children
     are Negroes. Their problems, pleasures, and moods are uni-
     versal. In trying to put herself on a child's level,
     Brooks "writes down" and falls into the commonplace.

4   ANON. Review of <u>Bronzeville Boys and Girls</u>, <u>SFC</u> (November 11),
     p. 23.
          It is a sensitive collection, and Ronni Solbert's draw-
     ings are among his best.

5   BISHOP, CLAIRE HUCHET. "A Selected List of Children's Books,"
     <u>Commonweal</u> (16 November), p. 181.
          Brooks sets the dreams and wonders of children into
     verse that is simple, moving, and rhythmical.

6   BRADLEY, VAN ALLEN. "Poetry Prize Winner Got an Early Start,"
     <u>CDN</u> (2 May).
          At 7 Brooks amazed her family by addressing them in
     rhymed speech. Now 32, she lives with her husband, Henry
     Blakely, a body and fender operator who writes. Their son,
     Henry, Jr., is 9. Brooks is a part-time assistant director
     at the South-Side Community Art Center. Currently, she is
     working on a volume of loosely collected pieces of fiction--
     "The Bronzeville Story."

8   LIBBY, MARGARET SHERWOOD. Review of <u>Bronzeville Boys and
     Girls</u>, <u>NYHTRB</u>, 33 (November 18).
          Each poem shows deep affection for youngsters. Although
     some verses are exquisite, others are light. The pieces
     are universal.

9   ROLLINS, CHARLEMAE. Review of <u>Bronzeville Boys and Girls</u>,
     <u>CST</u> (November 11), Sec. IV, p. 20.
          The volume is thoughtful and charming. Like Brooks's
     poetry for adults, this has realism but also gaiety and
     warmth. Ronni Solbert's drawings complement the verse.

1957 A BOOKS - NONE

1957

1957 B SHORTER WRITINGS

  1   ANON. Review of <u>Bronzeville Boys and Girls</u>, <u>Booklist</u>
         (January), p. 228.
            The collection is uneven but fresh. Although the chil-
         dren are Negro and the setting is Chicago, the experience
         of childhood is universal.

  2   ANON. "Jesuits' 100 Outstanding Chicagoans," <u>CST</u>
         (December 3), p. 18.
            The Jesuit Centennial Committee, chaired by Charles F.
         Murphy, screened more than 9,000 nominees and chose Brooks.
         <u>See also</u> 1950.B13.

  3   DERLETH, AUGUST. "A Varied Quartette," <u>Voices</u> (September-
         December), pp. 44-46.
            On <u>Bronzeville Boys and Girls</u>. Although Brooks's adult
         verse succeeds more than her poems for children, young
         readers should find much delight in the volume. Ronni
         Solbert's drawings are gratifying.

1958 A BOOKS - NONE

1958 B SHORTER WRITINGS

  1   ANON. "2 Chicago Poets to Appear February 12 in Loyola
         Series," <u>CST</u> (March 2).
            Henry Rago and Gwendolyn Brooks, two Chicago poets, will
         appear in Loyola University's David B. Steinman Visiting
         Poet series. Rago is editor of <u>Poetry</u>.

  2   ANON. "Language Arts Judges to Act in Difficult Field," <u>CDN</u>
         (May 20).
            Brooks is one of three prominent Chicagoans who will
         judge the <u>Chicago Daily News</u> nominees for the Silver Knight
         awards. Others are James H. McBurney, Dean of Speech at
         Northwestern University, and Dr. John P. Reich, former
         Professor of Dramatic Arts at Columbia University.

  3   POWERS, IRENE. "Cold Doesn't Deter Poets from Rounds," <u>CT</u>
         (February 12).
            In Lewis Towers at 8:00, Brooks and Henry Rago will read
         from their work. They will participate in a presentation
         by Loyola University. <u>A Street in Bronzeville</u> swept Brooks
         to fame, and <u>Annie Allen</u> won her the first Pulitzer ever
         awarded to a Negro.

1959 A BOOKS - NONE

1959 B SHORTER WRITINGS

1   BARDOLPH, RICHARD. <u>The Negro Vanguard</u>. New York: Holt,
      Rinehardt & Winston, pp. 279, 284.
          Like Hughes, Tolson, and Hayden, Gwendolyn Brooks suc-
      cessfully weathered the social changes between the forties
      and fifties.

2   HERGUTH, ROBERT. "Distinguished Panel to Select Top Youths,"
      <u>CDN</u> (March 23), p. 9.
          With the director of theater and the dean of a univer-
      sity's speech school, Brooks will help judge candidates for
      the Daily News Youth Achievement awards of 1959. She has
      an interest in teenagers.

1960 A BOOKS - NONE

1960 B SHORTER WRITINGS

1   ANON. "Poet Tells of Life in Bronzeville," <u>CST</u> (June 19).
          Brooks writes slowly and carefully, and tells about
      people who live in the slums. She has the basic ingredient
      of true artists--a deep compassion and a concern for human
      misery. Only a real poet can achieve the compactness of
      "A Bronzeville Mother," which combines a portrait of despair
      with an awakening of conscience.

2   ANON. Review of <u>The Bean Eaters</u>, <u>Booklist</u>, 56-57 (July 1),
      650.
          Many of the poems are well-wrought, strong, and broadly
      humanistic. A few, however, are painfully self-conscious
      and careless in technique.

3   ANON. Review of <u>The Bean Eaters</u>, <u>Bookmark</u> (April), p. 171.
          These fresh and incisive verses deal with commonplace
      situations and have disturbing undertones.

4   ANON. Review of <u>The Bean Eaters</u>, <u>KiR</u> (February 1), p. 131.
          Brooks's volume contributes highly to American poetry,
      as did her others. As always, her themes concern her
      people. Without self-pity or sentimentality, she writes
      with a deeply burning compassion. Although <u>The Bean Eaters</u>
      lacks the spontaneity of <u>A Street in Bronzeville</u>, it adds
      seriousness and maturity.

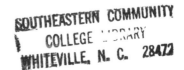

1960

5   BOCK, FREDERICK. "A Prize-Winning Poet Fails to Measure Up,"
    CST (Sunday Magazine, June 5), Sec. IV, p. 12.
        On The Bean Eaters. By now Brooks should have displayed
    a more controlled talent. Her glibness or smugness often
    undermine style and idea. Other qualities of her work are
    liveliness, easily sustained clarity, and satirical turn of
    fancy. Particularly regrettable is Brooks's complacent
    handling of many ambitious poems on racial themes.

6   BURKE, HERBERT. Review of The Bean Eaters, LJ, 85 (April 15),
    1599.
        Brooks is true to the "finest achievement in contempo-
    rary poetry." Her human and humane voice speaks with
    empathy. She touches the "universal pattern of suffering."

7   HARTMAN, GEOFFREY H. "Les Belles Dames Sans Merci," KeR, 22
    (Autumn), 691-700.
        On The Bean Eaters. Brooks's characters are either
    caught between small choices or big ones. "A Bronzeville
    Mother Loiters in Mississippi, Meanwhile a Mississippi
    Mother Burns Bacon" is the best poem. The ballads are good,
    but there are problems with a style that is folksy as well
    as sophisticated and runaway.

8   NATHAN, LEONARD E. "Four Books," Voices (September-December).
        On The Bean Eaters. Sometimes Brooks's impressionistic
    method is too elliptical or private and becomes obscure.
    The verses, however, have freshness and clarity. Since her
    technique works better in short poems, other verses ("Lovers
    of the Poor," "Bronzeville Mother...") are verbose or repe-
    titious. "We Real Cool" is too pat, and the point of view
    makes a judgment difficult.

9   PARKER, JOHN W. Review of The Bean Eaters, CLAJ (September 4),
    pp. 59-61.
        In The Bean Eaters, as elsewhere, Brooks's concerns are
    human fact and universal truth. Repetition of phrases and
    the absence of prepositions characterize her style. The
    Bean Eaters shows the "touch of an artist."

10 SHAPIRO, HARVEY. "A Quartet of Younger Singers," NYTBR, 23
    (October), 32.
        As in A Street in Bronzeville and Annie Allen, Brooks
    writes mainly about the Negro woman and the men of Bronze-
    ville. She discusses the plight of the Negro today. The
    poem about Little Rock has "some moving descriptions," but
    the "burden of theme is trite and the conclusion sentimen-
    tal." Similar triteness damages the few verses of social

satire. "The Ballad of Rudolph Reed" is better because its form and language contrast Negro life to the fictions of white culture. The shock is "immediate and lasting."

1961 A BOOKS - NONE

1961 B SHORTER WRITINGS

1   ANON. "Notes and Chatter," CDN (October 17).
         Late Friday afternoon, the board of Poetry met for an hour at Newberry Library to discuss plans for its poetry day celebration on November 13. They chose Brooks to read her works. Other choices were John Berryman, Denise Levertov, and William Stafford.

2   BROWN, FRANK LONDON. "Chicago's Great Lady of Poetry," ND, 10 (December), 53-57.
         Brooks is a "consummate artist." Her style reminds you of Virginia Woolf at her best; her complexity, of William Faulkner; her force and photographic clarity, of Thomas Wolfe. When Brooks received the notice that she had won the Pulitzer, the power company had turned off her lights because she could not pay her bill. In The Bean Eaters she utters one of the most piercing outcries against the murder of Emmett Till, but her rainbow is love.

3   DANA, ROBERT PATRICK. "Double Martini and Broken Crank Shaft," Prairie Schooner, 35 (Winter, 1961-62), 357-362.
         The Bean Eaters fails to equal A Street in Bronzeville and Annie Allen. "Callie Ford" and "Bronzeville Mother" only suggest the compelling book that might have been. Too often we find a breakdown of syntax and a strained use of nouns, verbs, and cliché.

4   FORD, NICK AARON. "Battle of the Books: A Critical Survey of Significant Books by and about Negroes Published in 1960," Phylon, 22 (Summer), 128-129.
         On The Bean Eaters. Brooks has displayed a strong feeling for irony and paradox, but these poems have little warmth. Some of them have titles that are strange and long. The pedantry and obscurity of Annie Allen does not appear. Brooks may be trying to exemplify T. S. Eliot's idea that poetry is an "escape from the emotions." In accordance with this philosophy, her success is admirable, but the philosophy itself is questionable.

1962

1962 A BOOKS - NONE

1962 B SHORTER WRITINGS

1   ANON. "Notes on a Poet," ND, 11 (August), 50, 76.
         Brooks is one of fifty poets invited to the National
     Poetry Festival, a symposium sponsored by the Library of
     Congress between October 22 and 24. Brooks will return
     home in order to lecture in American literature for three
     weeks in Chicago.

2   ANON. "Poet to Talk," CDN (December 5).
         At 1 p.m. Monday Brooks will speak in the library of the
     Crane campus, Chicago Teachers' College, 2240 W. Van Buren.

3   BRADLEY, VAN ALLEN. "Poetry Contest Judges Selected," CDN
     (July 23).
         Brooks is one. She joins Paul Engle, Director of the
     famous writers' workshop at the State University of Iowa,
     and Henry Rago, Chicago poet and editor of Poetry.

4   CHERRY, GWENDOLYN, RUBY THOMAS and PAULINE WILLIS. Portraits
     in Color. New York: Pageant Press.
         Biographical information. See 1950.B13.

5   DAVIS, ARTHUR P. "The Black and Tan Motif in the Poetry of
     Gwendolyn Brooks," CLAJ, 6 (December), 90-97.
         Brooks's poetry emphasizes a rejection based on color.
     Her poetry does not glorify blackness [undefined], for her
     dark girls are too realistic and disillusioned to find
     "solace in self-deception." She has written a new and
     subtler poetry of protest, but it is poetry and not polemic.

6   ETHRIDGE, JAMES M. Contemporary Authors. Detroit: Gale
     Research Co., the Book Tower, p. 36.
         This lists standard biographical information and gives
     the primary works up to The Bean Eaters. See 1950.B13.

7   SMITH, JOHN JUSTIN. "Chicago a Harbor for Anyone who Comes
     Here," CDN (April 28).
         Brooks's great heart accompanies her poetic gift.

8   WEBSTER, HARVEY CURTIS. "Pity the Gods," Nation (September 1),
     p. 967.
         The Bean Eaters surpasses A Street in Bronzeville,
     which surpasses Annie Allen. In engagement, Brooks re-
     sembles Langston Hughes, Countee Cullen, and Margaret

Walker; in ability to see through the temporal, Richard
Wright, James Baldwin, and Ralph Ellison. She uses the
rythms of blues less frequently than does Langston Hughes.
But she writes of the blessing, curse, and accident of
racial color. She "refuses to let Negro-ness limit her
humanity." Her best poems are those that concern the
Negro dilemma. The Bean Eaters has her most skillful
social poems. In "Bronzeville Mother...," point of view
is important, since the verse is written from the perspective of a white woman. Despite technical excellence, "The
Anniad" is diffuse and inferior. Her "crazy woman" poems
are "Yeats absorbed." Brooks ranks with the ablest of
modern poets.

9   _____. "The Poetry of Gwendolyn Brooks," CDN (October 13),
     p. 21.
          Reprint of 1962.B8.

1963 A BOOKS

1963 B SHORTER WRITINGS

1   ANON. "12 Arts Advisers Named by Kerner," CDN (August 24).
          Brooks participates in this effort to stimulate the
     arts.

2   ANON. "City Has Fifth of Nation's Most Influential Negroes,"
     CST (August 20), p. 14.
          Brooks has a poem, "The Sight of the Horizons," in the
     issue of Ebony that honors the centennial of the Emancipa-
     tion Proclamation.

3   ANON. "Joins Faculty," CDN (October 21), Sec. 2, p. 15.
          Brooks joins the faculty of Columbia College, 207 S.
     Wabash.

4   ANON. "Literary Notes," CST (October 29), p. 31.
          Brooks has joined the faculty of Columbia College. She
     will teach the techniques of poetry and the modern poets.

5   ANON. "Miss Brooks to Teach at Last," CDN (October 26).
          Brooks has agreed to teach at Columbia College, 207
     S. Wabash Avenue. When questioned about never having
     taught, she answers: "Because no one ever asked me....
     I guess because I have three strikes on me. I am a woman.
     I am Negro. And I have no college degree." Only in the
     minds of small men will these three matter.

1963

6   ANON. "Proclaim Saturday as 'Poetry Day,'" CST (November 14).
        In a picture, Mayor Daley hands a proclamation to Brooks.
    Augustine J. Bowe, Chief Justice of the Municipal Court,
    and Henry Rago, editor of Poetry, look on.

7   ANON. Review of Selected Poems, Booklist (October 15), p. 127.
        Besides her motif of the "Negro's place in American
    society," Brooks considers love and domestic scenes her
    favorite themes. The selections vary in depth and impact,
    but the best fuse sensibility with style.

8   ANON. Review of Selected Poems, LJ, 88 (Feburary), 4491.
        The verses deal with Negro life and contemporary prob-
    lems but the vividness and compassion are universal.

9   ADAMS, RUSSELL L. Great Negroes Past and Present. Chicago:
    Afro-American Publishing Co., p. 128.
        Nothing about Brooks's appearance suggests that she is
    one of America's greatest poets. By studying technique
    and social milieu, she creates "superb poetic renditions
    of urban Negro life." She has written some of the "finest
    poetry of our time." See also 1950.B13.

10 BARROW, WILLIAM. "On Black Women," ND, 12 (July), 78-83.
        Like Brooks's poems, Maud Martha is simple in structure.
    Although it is spare or small, its statement of the human
    condition is profoundly moving.

11 BERQUIST, RONALD. "Expect 1,200 to Attend Enlarged Book-
    Author Luncheon," CST (September 26), p. 6.
        Brooks will attend, and others will speak: Ben Hart,
    a journalist; Mark Van Doren, a poet; and John Mason Brown,
    a drama critic.

12 BRADLEY, VAN ALLEN. "'Chicago Poem' Jury at Work," CDN
    (June 8), p. 11.
        Brooks will help to decide the recipient of the $1,000
    prize for the poem that best expresses the meaning of
    Chicago in the modern world. Other participants are Paul
    Engle, Director of the State University of Iowa's writers'
    workshop, and Henry Rago, editor of Poetry. Harper and
    Row schedules Brooks's Selected Poems for publication in
    August.

13 _____. "Our Recognizing Our Writers," CDN (April 6).
        In fifteen years neither Gwendolyn Brooks nor Nelson
    Algren, two authors of international reputation, has ever
    received major recognition from a giver of local prizes.

Is there a maxim about a prophet "without honor in his own
country"? Along with Paul Engle and Henry Rago, Brooks is
judging a poetry contest. The purpose is to determine the
poem that best expresses the meaning and spirit of contemporary Chicago. Engle is a distinguished poet and Rago is
the editor of Poetry.

14 CUTLER, BRUCE. "A Long Reach, Strong Speech," Poetry, 103
    (October-March), 387-393.
        On Selected Poems. Brooks is one of the "very best
    poets." She can make the spoken language work as verse.
    With comprehension and ease, she can handle topical subject
    matter, as in "The Chicago Defender Sends a Man to Little
    Rock." Her width of technique ranges from aphorisitc
    rhyme to an imagery of intense empathy.

15 DUFFY, JOHN. "Style and Exasperation," Spirit, 30-31 (1963-65),
    47-48.
        On Selected Poems. Gwendolyn Brooks has style--the
    style of inspired speech that is profoundly impassioned but
    precisely controlled. She is very serious about the Negro
    question.

16 ENGLE, PAUL. "Miss Brooks: City's Laureate," CT
    (September 22), p. 2.
        Brooks's lyrical voice continues shaping itself, as does
    the City of Chicago. With a candid eye, Brooks balances
    the savage and the sentimental. Her verses have different
    moods of delight and toughness. She recreates insight, and
    her talent is as "genuine as light itself."

17 GLAUBER, ROBERT H. "Our Miss Brooks: Lyricist," CST
    (September 22).
        Since 1945, Brooks has interwoven biting social criti-
    cism into her verse, but poetry has always been her prime
    concern.

18 MENN, THORPE. "Major National Prize Winners to Poetry
    Series," KCS (September 9).
        Brooks is the last in a series of five poets to perform
    at a local Jewish Community Center. Others are William A.
    Stafford, Karl Shapiro, Dan Jaffe, and Donald Drummond.

19 MORSE, CARL. "All Have Something to Say," NYTBR (October 6).
        On Selected Poems. The volume is a pleasure to read,
    since Brooks's heart is warm, and her head is cool. The
    poet never fails to distinguish between the sad and the

1963

silly. Occasionally she is too sentimental or becomes too
involved with furniture or ephemera, but these do not under-
mine the general impression. Brooks deserved the Pulitzer
prize that she won in 1950.

20 NYREN, DOROTHY. Review of Selected Poems, LJ, 88 (July),
2708.
The lyrics are direct, simple, and pleasantly feminine.

21 SIMPSON, LOUIS. "Don't Take a Poem by the Horns," Bookweek
(October 27), pp. 6, 26.
On Selected Poems. It contains some "lively pictures
of Negro life." Although a Negro might not be able to
write well without revealing her race, the writing is unimportant if being a Negro is the only subject. It must
have been difficult for Brooks to write poetry in America
where one hardly ever finds any Negro poetry worth discus-
sing. Her seriousness is praiseworthy, but one should
criticize her into writing more poems like "The Bean Eaters."

1964 A BOOKS - NONE

1964 B SHORTER WRITINGS

1 ANON. "Depres to Talk Here at College Commencement," CST
(June 16).
Brooks, a faculty member at Columbia College, will be
presented an honorary Doctorate of Humane Letters. Leon M.
Depres, commencement speaker, has as his subject "America's
20th Century Frontier--the City." The ceremony is 8:00
Tuesday night.

2 ANON. "An Evening with the Poets," CST (November 12).
At Orchestra Hall, on Friday evening, five of the na-
tion's best-known younger poets will read: John Berryman,
Denise Levertov, William Stafford, Gwendolyn Brooks, and
Henry Rago. The occasion is Poetry Day Concert, the tenth
annual benefit program for Poetry.

3 NO ENTRY

4 ANON. "Front Row Center," CST (April 2).
At its annual awards dinner, the Friends of Literature
give $100, the Robert F. Ferguson Memorial prize, to Brooks
for her Selected Poems.

5 ANON. "55 Good Citizen Awards Given Out by Local Unit," CST
   (April 2), p. 34.
        Brooks receives one.

6 ANON. "Gwendolyn Brooks," CST (July 3).
        Brooks will be on the program of a summer conference on
   "The Negro Writer in the United States," presented by the
   University of California Extension at Pacific Grove, on
   the North California Coast, August 5-9.

7 ANON. "Honor 31 Leaders as Good Americans," CDN (April 2).
        Brooks wins an award.

8 ANON. "Miss Brooks and Depres Honored by College Here," CST
   (June 17).
        At Columbia College's graduation exercises, in the
   Prudential Building, Gwendolyn Brooks and Leon M. Depres
   were awarded honorary degrees Tuesday night.

9 ANON. "Name Scientist, Poet to Student Grants Agency," CST
   (October 13).
        The Institute of International Education has announced
   that Gwendolyn Brooks and scientist Dr. Percy Julian have
   been appointed to its committee of Midwest Regional
   advisers.

10 ANON. "Negro Author Gets Degree at Columbia," CDN (July 17).
        Tuesday night, during graduation ceremonies at Columbia
   College, Brooks received a Doctorate of Humane Letters.
   According to Mirron Alexandroff, Columbia President, she
   was honored for "celebrated contributions to American
   letters."

11 ANON. "Notes," CDN (May 5).
        At his home, Gordon Monsens will give a late evening
   supper Thursday for Brooks. Earlier she will speak with
   some students of Barrington High.

12 ANON. "Notes on People and Occurrences," CST (May 27).
        Like Harry Petrakis, Brooks, of Chicago's Columbia
   College, won a major award from the Society of Midland
   Authors.

13 ANON. "Poetry's Impact on Public Stressed," CDN (November 13).
        Brooks attends a conference that focuses on the relevancy
   of poetry and its importance in shaping human values. Others
   attending are Henry Rago, William Stafford, Denise Levertov,
   and John Berryman.

1964

14 ANON. "Poetry Winners Named," KCT (April 17).
    At a local Jewish Community Center last night, Brooks
    presented checks to three winners in the Heart of America
    Poetry Contests. Her droll wit drew applause, as did some
    of her more serious poems. The Kansas City Star award of
    $100 for a poem submitted in open competition went to Bruce
    Cutler of Wichita.

15 ANON. "Prize-Winning Poet Will Get College Honor," CT
    (June 14), Sec. 1, p. 27.
    Brooks will receive an honorary doctorate of humane let-
    ters at Columbia College Commencement exercises, 8 p.m.,
    Tuesday, in the Prudential Building auditorium.

16 ANON. "Pulitzer Poet to Lecture at Northwestern University on
    Mid-Century American Poets," CDD, 27 (June), p. 16.
    Brooks will be one of six guest lecturers at a symposium
    on "Interpretation of Mid-Century American Writers" at
    Northwestern University, June 29 through August 22. Other
    participants are Allen Seager, Professor of English at the
    University of Michigan and internationally known novelist
    and short story writer; Lee Anderson, Research Associate
    in English at Yale University and Coordinator of the Yale
    Series of Recorded Poets; Glenna Syse, drama critic and
    columnist for the Chicago Sun Times; Charles McGraw,
    Senior Director of Drama (institution unlisted); and Robert
    Sickinger, Director of Hull House Theater. See also 1950.B13.

17 ANON. "Society of Midland Authors Makes 1963 Book Awards,"
    CST (May 23).
    At a dinner Friday night, Brooks received the $500
    Thormond L. Monsen award for her book Selected Poems.

18 ANON. "Tell It Like It Is," Newsweek, 64 (July-September),
    84-85.
    Although Brooks is present at a writer's conference on
    the west coast, Ellison and Baldwin are considered the two
    Negro writers of the most importance.

19 AUSTIN, DOROTHY WITTE. "Poetry Enriches Life, Woman Finds,"
    MJ (May 24), Part 6, p. 2.
    Brooks's favorite was not Annie Allen but A Street in
    Bronzeville. She calls Annie Allen rather pretentious and
    excessively decorated, but says that it was a time of
    growth.

20 BAUR, LOIS. "Literary Agents' Party Talk of Town," CA
    (June 3), Sec. 2, p. 9.

Brooks said quietly that she had no special time for
writing poetry. Throughout the party she stood in the same
spot. Sometimes she spoke with a secret smile or a sadness.

21   CROMIE, ROBERT. "Looks at Authors and Books," CT (June 9).
Recently awarded an honorary Doctorate of Humane Letters
from Columbia College, Brooks contemplates a book of child-
hood reminiscences. Once she won the Pulitzer Prize.

22   FAHERDT, ROBERT. "Literature in Chicago," CDN (May 23).
At a dinner at the Sheraton Chicago last night, Brooks
won the Thormond L. Monsen $500 award for her Selected
Poems. Only a few weeks ago she received another local
prize.

23   FORD, NICK AARON. "The Fire Next Time? A Critical Survey of
Belles Lettres by and about Negroes," Phylon, 25 (Summer),
132.
Although the new verses are in the style and vision which
won the Pulitzer in 1950, there is more warmth and less
pedantry or obscurity. Only in "Riders to the Blood Red
Wrath" does one find the cold artificiality of Annie Allen.

24   FULLER, HOYT W. "The Negro Writer in the United States."
Ebony (November), pp. 126-128, 134.
Louis Simpson (1963.B21) failed to perceive the universality in Negro life. Despite people like him, a distinguished
conference took place on August 5. When reading their poetry, Gwendolyn Brooks and LeRoi Jones became aware of tension in the audience. The participants strongly favored
one style or the other. The two writers, however, displayed
a rare and respectful deference to each other.

25   HEDLUND, MARILOU. "How Noted Poets Spin Verses," CT
(November 13).
Gwendolyn Brooks and Henry Rago, both Chicagoans, write
for different reasons, and their poetry is different.
Brooks writes in the mornings. Housekeeping means nothing
to her, since she turns attention to house chores after
having done some writing. Rago writes late at night.
Brooks writes about the Negro whom she knows best. Both
Rago and Brooks will read verses during the tenth annual
celebration of Poetry at 8:30 tonight in Orchestra Hall.
Other readers will be John Berryman, Denise Levertov, and
William Stafford.

26   JAFFE, DOROTHEA KAHN. "A Poem, No Propaganda," CSM (March 25).
To the question of whether she writes a poetry of protest, Brooks replies: "I have always written about justice

1964

in human relations.... But no matter what the theme is, I still want the poem to be a poem and not just a piece of propaganda." Her verses and Maud Martha make one understand the Negro quest for equal rights. Marriage and motherhood did not interrupt Brooks's career.

27 REXROTH, KENNETH. "Panelizing Dissent," The Nation, 199 (September 7), 97-99.

LeRoi Jones and Gwendolyn Brooks stand at opposite ends of American literature, but the audience was attentive to both at the Black Writers' Conference (August 5-9) which took place in one of the California State Parks. Under the auspices of the Letters and Science Extension, the program received support as part of the Special Programs of the University of California. Herbert Hill, Secretary of the NAACP, was General Manager. Noting the liberal aid from foundations, one can see that dissent and revolt have become institutionalized. Three programs raised a genuine and literary response: Brooks's reading, Jones's reading, and Arna Bontemps's talk on Jean Toomer and the Harlem Renaissance.

28 RIVERS, CONRAD KENT. "The Poetry of Gwendolyn Brooks," ND, 13 (June), 67-68.

Brooks is a prophet and a brooder, and her poetry ranks with the best produced in America. She is a "disciple of truth." Beneath the didacticism of her verse lies a heart of controlled hate and full love.

29 SPECTOR, ROBERT S. "The Poet's Other Voices, Other Poems," SatR, 47 (February 1), 36-38.

On Selected Poems. Tenderness underlies the indignation at racism. The power of anger and sympathy go deeper than race. A technical proficiency of blues and ballads exists, but Brooks's ability to empathize and to create empathy make her a poet.

1965 A BOOKS - NONE

1965 B SHORTER WRITINGS

*1 BANWICK, MARY BETH. "Pulitzer Prize Winner Joins Lecture Staff," Interim, 2 (February 24), 1.

Unlocatable. Listed in Loff (1973.B6).

2 MORAN, RONALD. "Time of Heterogeneity," SoR, 1, 473-485. 473-485.

1966

Brooks's personal tradition is one of relentless vigor
and impressive insistence. Her most successful poems are
psychological and sociological studies in the American city.

1966 A BOOKS

1   CLYDE, GLENDA E. An Oral Interpreter's Approach to the Poetry
    of Gwendolyn Brooks. Carbondale: Doctoral Dissertation,
    Southern Illinois University.
        The purpose of this study is to examine the poetry of
    Gwendolyn Brooks in order to discover: (1) the unique
    characteristics and elements of importance in her verse and
    (2) an analytical method or approach that would facilitate
    the oral interpretation, preparation, and presentation of
    her verse. The concerns are the development of the speak-
    ing voice in the poem, point of view, nature of speaker,
    dramatic situation, and nature of the speaker's involvement.

1966 B SHORTER WRITINGS

1   ANON. The Negro in American Literature and Bibliography by
    and About Negro Americans. Oshkosh, Wisconsin: Wisconsin
    Council of Teachers of English. Non-circulating and rare.
        This lists works by genre. Under novels one will find
    Maud Martha; under poetry, all of Brooks's volumes up to
    Selected Poems (1963).

2   LITTLEJOHN, DAVID. "Negro Writers Today: The Novelists: II,"
    in Black on White: A Critical Survey of Writing by American
    Negroes. New York: Viking, pp. 89-94.
        By being dedicated to craft, Brooks is more a poet than
    a Negro. She demonstrates a greater degree of artistic
    control than any other American Negro writer. Among Negro
    practitioners only LeRoi Jones demands the same degree of
    poetic respect, for the two have a similar seriousness of
    purpose and intensity of modern idiom. Since Jones engages
    in anti-verbal expressions, however, and Brooks in the sub-
    limation of problems to craft, the writers exist at differ-
    ent extremes. In the early poems, Brooks's love is words
    per se, not things or people. Sections VII and XV (Annie
    Allen) of "The Womanhood" give admirable control to a
    seething and racial intensity of statement, although the
    volume is mandarin. The latter section is impressive for
    its statement on latent Jim Crowism. It is also a real
    artist's contribution to the "Negro War Fund." Brooks is
    too aloof to be useful in this racial war. By her pains-
    taking and exquisite art, she has passed through battle.

1966

3   MILLER, ELIZABETH.   The Negro in America: A Bibliography.
    Cambridge: Harvard University Press, p. 39.
        This mainly lists Brooks's works and their publishers
    up to Selected Poems (1963).   It provides generic designa-
    tion.   To A Street in Bronzeville there is a descriptive
    note: "Poems which convey with great success the authentic
    flavor of Negro community life in Chicago."

1968 A BOOKS - NONE

1968 B SHORTER WRITINGS

1   ANON.   Review of In the Mecca, Booklist, 64-65 (October 15),
    223-224.
        Major qualities characterize the inhabitants of the
    Mecca building and Brooks's shorter poems: clarity, dig-
    nity, humor, and drama.

2   ANON.   Review of In the Mecca, Booklist, 64-65 (November 1),
    298.
        This is dramatic poetry that reflects contemporary
    urban life.

3   EMANUEL, JAMES A. and THEODORE L. GROSS.   Dark Symphony.   New
    York: Free Press, p. 499.
        In a Petrarchan sonnet such as "First Fight," Brooks can
    fuse violin music with complex allusions.   In "The Egg
    Boiler," another sonnet, she briefly echoes Keats and Frost.
    Brooks places literary beauty and truth above utilitarian
    fact.   See also 1950.B13.

4   FULLER, HOYT W.   "Towards a Black Aesthetic," The Black
    Aesthetic.   Edited by Addison Gayle, Jr.   New York:
    Anchor Books, pp. 3-11.
        Taking issue with the white critical establishment, the
    writer cites 1963.B21:   "All the history of American race
    relations is contained in that appraisal, despite its dis-
    ingenuousness.   It is civilized, urbane, gentle and elegant;
    and it is arrogant, condescending, presumptious and racist."

5   GARLAND, PHYL.   "Gwendolyn Brooks: Poet Laureate," Ebony
    (July), pp. 48-49.
        After walking out of a Chicago Arts Conference, young
    writers come to Brooks's modest home.   It is ironic that
    they seek Gwendolyn Brooks, part of the same cultural "es-
    tablishment" from which they have claimed independence.
    They know that she agrees with their literary quests, their

need to chart their own way. One admirer says that Brooks's
statements may seem quiet, but she has always dealt with
reality. Young writers think of her as a bridge. <u>See also</u>
1950.B13.

1969 A BOOKS - NONE

1969 B SHORTER WRITINGS

1 ANON. Review of <u>In the Mecca</u>, <u>VQR</u>, 45 (Winter), 20.
       Brooks is more self-consciously a Negro than ever before.
   In the face of despair, she gives a sermon of life. The
   manner and the voice are new. If the honesty is better
   than before, the music and control are poorer. The change
   indicates that the poet is still alive.

2 BENSON, BRIAN J. Review of <u>In the Mecca</u>, <u>CLAJ</u>, 13 (December),
       203.
       Her ability to portray the passionate Negro is strongly
   evident. In "The Chicago Picasso," one finds the "most
   starkly beautiful description." Her eye is keen, her sense
   perceptive, and her pen graphic. Each verse has an intrin-
   sic symbolism, although she uses wide-ranging symbolism
   sparingly and carefully. She has sharpened her sensibilities
   to the tunes fashioned by young Negro intellectuals.

3 BIRD, G. LEONARD. "Gwendolyn Brooks: Educator Extraordinaire,"
       <u>Discourse</u>, 12 (Spring), 158-166.
       <u>In the Mecca</u> is a microcosm both of the Black community
   and the human one. DuBois perceived a duality of consciousness in Blacks--racial and rational. No black has "more
   successfully or vividly rendered those ambiguities than
   Gwendolyn Brooks." Some of Mrs. Smith's neighbors--
   St. Julia Jones, Prophet Williams, Alfred--epitomize the
   spiritual isolation of the ghetto dweller. Although
   Brooks's characters and setting are Negro, her private
   truth "corresponds to the public truth of our age." If
   the dramatic situation is Negro, the theme is universal
   humanity.

4 BONTEMPS, ARNA. "Negro Poets Then and Now," in <u>Black Expres-
       sion</u>. Edited by Addison Gayle, Jr. New York: Weybright
   and Tally, pp. 82-89.
       Brooks has received the "most substantial critical
   approval" of the post-Renaissance group of Negro poets in
   the U.S.

1969

5   DAVIS, ARTHUR P.   "Poet of the Unheroic," <u>CLAJ</u>, 7 (December), 114-125.
        For Brooks the modern world is unheroic. She has no knowledge of Négritude. Presumably the poems discussed concern Bronzeville citizens, but almost nothing about them suggests that the characters portrayed are Negroes. Like James Joyce, she writes about a nationality or group so humanly that restrictive considerations are forgotten. Her qualities are irony, humor, and pity. Her words are usually not fiery, defiant, or bitter. In <u>A Street in Bronzeville</u>, <u>Annie Allen</u>, or <u>In the Mecca</u>, Rudolph Reed may be the one heroic figure. But even he is "just a plain man goaded to violence by an attack on his home." Brooks's poems lack any glorification of the idea that Black is beautiful because her suffering girls choose realism over self-deception. She lacks any faith in the American Dream or in a just God. Often she writes clearly, but she can be modern or difficult, as in "The Anniad." Whether using colloquial or involved styles, she is rewarding.

6   EMANUEL, JAMES A.   "The Future of Negro Poetry," in <u>Black Expression</u>. Edited by Addison Gayle, Jr. New York: Weybright and Tally, pp. 105-107.
        Brooks's fourth sonnet from <u>Annie Allen</u> and Claude McKay's "White House" deserve the formalistic analysis merited by the best Negro poetry.

7   JAFFE, DAN.   "Gwendolyn Brooks: An Appreciation from the White Suburbs," in <u>The Black American Writer</u>. Edited by C. W. E. Bigsby. Deland, Florida: Everett/Edwards, pp. 89-98.
        On <u>Annie Allen</u>. Brooks has not forsaken the muse for the cause, and her work shows a concern for craft. Although she may not have written her major poems yet, she has done some verses that people will read as long as concern for language and humanity survive. Never, perhaps, will critics speak of an early or late Brooks. Her tactics and subjects show no great changes over the years, but one does find a "steady development of themes and types." By technical dexterity, her poems become experiences rather than ideas. The section entitled "The Womanhood" includes "some of the best poems by any contemporary American poet." Brooks's lesson is keeping sensitivity alive in a world of brutality or destruction.

8   LAING, ALEXANDER.   "The Politics of Poetry," <u>The Nation</u>, 209 (July 7), 2628.
        <u>In the Mecca</u> is political, but it verifies Brooks's "impressive growth into a new prosody."

114

9   RANDALL, DUDLEY. "Black Poetry," in Black Expression. Edited
     by Addison Gayle, Jr. New York: Weybright and Tally,
     p. 114.
        In the Mecca suggests Brooks's association in her work-
     shop with militant young Chicago South-Side writers. There
     are still the precise, glittering, and startling phrases,
     but there are fewer "feminine" epithets. Certain passages
     have a raw power that overwhelms. One finds violence, hor-
     hor, and tragedy as well as a piercing insight into people's
     minds.

10 ROSENTHAL, M. L. "In the Mecca," NYTBR (March 2), p. 14.
        The title poem is overwrought with effects--alliteration,
     internal rhymes, whimsical and arch observations--that
     "distract from its horror almost as if to conceal the wound
     at its center."

11 STAFFORD, WILLIAMS. "Books That Look Out, Books That Look In,"
     Poetry, 113 (March), 421-425.
        On In the Mecca. This dedicates a paragraph to Brooks--
     the least coverage of five poets. "She writes with the con-
     fidence and momentum of a tradition that intends to be
     established...." She chooses reality over falsity and does
     not abandon judgment. The result is complexity. Sometimes
     the poems are confusingly local, but their strong feelings
     surface abruptly. A steady view or insight is implied
     throughout.

12 TOPPIN, EDGAR A. A Biographical History of Blacks in America
     Since 1528. New York: David McKay.
        Brooks's poetry "brilliantly evokes Northern ghetto life
     and universalizes human experience in contemporary garb."
     Until now Brooks is the only Afro-American to win the
     Pulitzer Prize.

1970 A BOOKS - NONE

1970 B SHORTER WRITINGS

1   DAVIS, CHARLES T. and DANIEL WALDEN, ed. "Gwendolyn Brooks,"
     in On Being Black. Greenwich: Fawcett, p. 379.
        In the 1940's Brooks's first critical recognition came
     at Northwestern University Writers' Conferences. As a poet,
     she has used traditional forms in unconventional ways. Her
     incisive but individual poems have made her both an admired
     poet and a spokesman for her race.

1970

2   DRONTING, PHILLIP T. and WESLEY W. SOUTH. <u>Up From the Ghetto</u>.
     New York: Cowles Book, Inc., pp. 170-176.
             From her beginnings in Kansas, Brooks went on to literary
     stardom in Chicago. In 1969, she "went natural." The
     writing in poems such as <u>Riot</u> is taking a more militant
     tone. Two years ago Brooks succeeded Carl Sandburg as
     "Poet Laureate of Illinois." She always encourages young
     black writers.

3   JOHNSON, THOMAS A. "Yale Conference Studies Role of Black
     Women," <u>NYT</u> (December 14), p. 45.
             Brooks reads from her own works and from works by other
     black women poets. She announces that Broadside, a black
     publishing firm, will print her work from now on. She has
     an opinion concerning women's liberation: "Our black men
     have enough to do without worrying about black women either
     getting behind or in front of them."

4   MILLER, JEANNE-MARIE A. "Gwendolyn Brooks--Poet Laureate of
     Bronzeville, U.S.A.," <u>Freedomways</u>, 10 (1st Quarter), 63-75.
             Although her idiom is local, her language is universal.
     The tones and forms are varied, the imagery exact, and the
     diction crisp.

*5   RANDALL, DUDLEY. "On Getting a Natural," Broadside Poster.
     Unlocatable. Cited in Loff (1973.B6).

6   RAY, DAVID, ed. "Gwendolyn Brooks," in <u>Contemporary Poets of
     the English Language</u>. New York: St. Martins Press,
     pp. 139-141.
             The methodology allows for a listing of primary works up
     to <u>In the Mecca</u> (1968) and of anthologies in which Brooks's
     work appears up to 1965. In America Brooks is one of the
     "most accomplished poets." Through her a minority's reality
     becomes the world's. Like Wallace Stevens, she has a deep
     and imaginative penetration, an ingenuity for satire. For
     a world in which poetry has too often become esoteric, she
     returns the reader to the reality of life. She is one of
     the "most <u>objective</u> poets writing in the United States."
     <u>See</u> 1950.B13.

7   ROBINSON, DONALD, ed. "Gwendolyn Brooks," in <u>The 100 Most
     Important People in the World Today</u>. New York: G. P.
     Putnam's Sons, pp. 321-323.
             Brooks's work has the timeless elegance that makes for
     fine poetry. It communicates the grim reality of tenement
     and street.

8   WARREN, MARR, II. "Black Pulitzer Awardees," Crisis, 77
     (May), 186-188.
         Brooks is one of three blacks to win the Pulitzer. The
     other two are Charles Gordone for drama, No Place to Be
     Somebody (1969), and Monata J. Sleet, Jr., for his work as
     a photographer with Johnson publications. See also
     1950.B13.

1971 A BOOKS - NONE

1971 B SHORTER WRITINGS

1   ANON. "Artists, Friends, Admirers Gather in Tribute to
     Poetess Gwendolyn Brooks," Jet, 39 (February 25), 16-17.
         With the aid of Johnson Publishing Company, more than
     sixty writers gathered their work. The purpose was to
     produce a book of tributes, To Gwen With Love. Dramatist
     Val Gray and writer Patricia L. Brown headed the project.

2   ANON. "Books for Young Adults," Booklist, 67-68 (December),
     327.
         On The World of Gwendolyn Brooks. High School libraries
     should have this text, since it is a comprehensive collec-
     tion of a recognized black poet's works.

3   ANON. "Brooks, Gwendolyn," Who's Who in American Women.
     Chicago: Kingsport Press.
         Biographical information. See 1950.B13.

4   BENNET, LERONE, JR. "Introduction," in To Gwen With Love.
     Edited by Patricia L. Brown, Don L. Lee, and Francis Ward.
     Chicago: Johnson Publishing Company, pp. 1-3.
         Brooks has always written about the Black Community. By
     celebrating her personal truth, her verses celebrate the
     truth of blackness [undefined] and of man. Brooks has been
     lyrical and relevant. An overwhelming concreteness is one
     of her greatest virtues.

5   BURROUGHS, MARGARET T. "She'll Speak to Generations Yet to
     Come," in To Gwen With Love. Edited by Patricia L. Brown,
     Don L. Lee, and Francis Ward. Chicago: Johnson Publishing
     Company, p. 130.
         Brooks's poetry will speak to generations yet unborn.
     Humanity is her concern, and she can shape her individual
     experience until it expresses the universals of all the
     downtrodden and oppressed.

1971

6   GIOVANNI, NIKKI. "For Gwen Brooks," Essence (April), p. 26.
         I first encountered the poetry of Brooks at Austin High
     in Knoxville, Tennessee, and I understood Annie Allen to be
     my mother. I gave up Ginsburg for "We Real Cool."

7   KENT, GEORGE E. "Notation Concerning the World of Gwendolyn
     Brooks," Booklist, 67-68 (November 15), 277.
         Lists the contents of her previous volumes, but enters
     no critical opinion.

8   _____. "The Poetry of Gwendolyn Brooks, Part I," BlackW, 20
     (September), 30-43.
         Brooks's depth of responsiveness and range in poetry
     distinguish her as one of the ablest American poets of this
     century. Like Langston Hughes, she was sensitive to the
     changes in the Black community during different decades.
     In the 1960's the title poem of In the Mecca was the deepest
     verse that portrayed the "hopelessness of urban Blacks."
     As a modern poet, she is widely read. A Street in Bronze-
     ville, her first volume, is a favorite among Blacks. Al-
     though her verse reflects the influence of white moderns
     such as Pound and Eliot, it draws no less upon Black writers
     such as Hughes. Narrative distance, gentle satire, and
     calm humor give to Brooks individual sensitivity and
     value. Her techniques are irony, unusual conjunctions, a
     complex sense of reality, sudden contrasts, condensation of
     image, lyrical sensitivity, and experimentation. By going
     down deeply, rather than transcending, she reaches univer-
     salism. A religious consciousness without dogma is a source
     for her sensibility. See 1971.B9.

9   _____. "The Poetry of Gwendolyn Brooks, Part II," BlackW, 20
     (October), 36-48.
         Her verse places her in the front rank of Black American
     poets. "The Mother," however, suffers from a labored irony
     in which the narrator fails to convey her attitude toward
     the subject. "A Bronzeville Mother..." arrives at the uni-
     versal too soon, since its resolution requires that a
     greater basis of logic be found in earlier parts of the
     text. In the Mecca, Riot, and Family Pictures represent
     the poet's responses to a changing Black community, and
     one should read them together. "Children of the Poor"
     is the most masterful description in poetry of the Black
     Mother's dilemma; it is one of the most memorable and
     rhythmic pieces in the English language. "The Anniad,"
     like "In the Mecca," deserves its own analysis. Brooks has
     helped this author analyse the former. The latter becomes
     "one of those very terrible wastelands that jump forth with

vitality at each reading." In style, part of its success
comes from an easy movement between colloquial and formal
manners. If Brooks cannot move directly into the Southern
past, as do Langston Hughes and Margaret Walker, she gives
an intensity that makes the past alive in the present.
See also 1971.B8.

10   McPHERSON, JAMES M., et al. Blacks in America. Garden City:
     Doubleday, p. 249.
         This entry is bibliographical. In paragraph form it
     lists Brooks's primary volumes, from A Street in Bronzeville
     to In the Mecca. Secondary articles on the poet range from
     Stanley Kunitz's "Bronze by Gold" (1950.B21) to George
     Starvros's interview (1970).

11   SKEETER, SHARYN J. Review of Family Pictures, Essence, 2
     (June), 72.
         With compassion and understanding, Brooks writes about
     young people.

12   WARD, FRANCIS. "Home Has Always Been Blackness," in To Gwen
     With Love. Edited by Patricia L. Brown, Don L. Lee, and
     Francis Ward. Chicago: Johnson Publishing Company,
     pp. 31-32.
         Not you, Gwen, but black people have changed; you have
     only regenerated. With sincerity of identity, you withstood
     affection and hypocrisy, the honor of Poet Laureate, and
     the Pulitzer Prize. You retained constancy, humility, and
     devotion, both to your art and to black people. Creating
     a new humanity "has been your work ever since this land
     was blessed with your genius..."

1972 A BOOKS

1   LOFF, JON N. To Be a Black Woman in the Poetry of Gwendolyn
     Brooks. Steven's Point: Master's Thesis: University of
     Wisconsin, 66 pp.
         The chapters are "Gwendolyn Brooks: Poet Laureate of
     the Poor"; "Notes from Childhood and Girlhood"; "Womanhood";
     "Motherhood"; and "Conclusion." Brooks studied the styles
     of many poets such as James Weldon Johnson, Langston Hughes,
     Paul Laurence Dunbar, T. S. Eliot, and Countee Cullen. But
     she studied their language and techniques "only to improve
     her own artistic ability." Her purpose is to understand
     and describe the dilemmas of Black women who grow up in the
     ghetto. Brooks's poems about the Black female reflect the
     gamut of human emotions: discontent, futility, desire,
     fear, courage, and despair.

1972

2   SHAW, HARRY BERNARD. <u>Social Themes in the Poetry of Gwendolyn
     Brooks</u>. Urbana: Doctoral Dissertation, the University of
     Illinois.
          Chapters are as follows: "Introduction"; "Death"; "The
     Fall from Glory"; "The Labyrinth"; "Survival"; and "Conclu-
     sion." The themes in Brooks's verse constitute a nemesis
     of black life. The order of discussion here parallels that
     of their introduction in the body of the writer's work.
     Brooks first depicts the Black man's reality as spiritual
     death. She then shows that the Black man views his former
     glory and freedom from this vantage point. The poetry fo-
     cuses next on the Black man's hell in the United States--
     the labyrinth. Finally, one finds the theme of survival.
     With its components of restraint, militance, and rebirth,
     this motif offers an alternative: by endurance the Black
     man can solve the labyrinth and reclaim former glory.

<u>1972 B SHORTER WRITINGS</u>

1   BAKER, HOUSTON A., JR. "The Achievement of Gwendolyn Brooks,"
     <u>CLAJ</u>, 16 (Fall), 23-31.
          Although many of her techniques and themes place Brooks
     in the mainstream of Twentieth Century Poetry, others root
     her firmly in a Black American literary tradition. Like
     other poets of her time, she considers the terrors of war.
     An effective technique from the Black tradition is a sharp
     and comic irony that resembles Langston Hughes's tone in
     <u>The Ways of White Folks</u>. While Brooks employs polysyllables,
     she preserves colloquial rhythms, and only the best of
     Robert Frost equals her work in this style. If her form
     is white, her content is black. Reprinted 1974.B1.

2   CULLEN, COUNTEE. "August 24, 1945," in <u>Report from Part One</u>.
     Edited by Gwendolyn Brooks. Detroit: Broadside Press,
     p. 201.
          Having just finished the reading of <u>A Street in Bronze-
     ville</u>, I want you to know that I enjoyed it completely.
     You are a good poet who gives every indication of becoming
     better.

3   GAYLE, ADDISON, JR. "Making Beauty from Racial Anxiety,"
     <u>NYTBR</u> (January 2), p. 420.
          On <u>The World of Gwendolyn Brooks</u>. Brooks presents old
     truths in new trappings. Behind the mask of philosopher
     poet, she keeps the face of an Afro-American who has humane
     sensibility. These works show a firm control of technique
     and form and reflect a growth in the poet's awareness.
     When evaluated by such criteria, Brooks surpasses most of

her contemporaries. In <u>The Bean Eaters</u> "The Ballad of
Rudolph Reed" is "most compelling." The faults of Brooks's
work lie in a childish fascination for words. At some
point her images should communicate.

4   HANSELL, WILLIAM HAROLD. "Positive Themes in the Poetry of
Four Negroes," <u>DA</u> (University of Wisconsin), 33 (July),
p. 754A.
Cited in <u>DA</u>. In Brooks's verse, one finds the culmina-
tion of three qualities: Claude McKay's independence and
personal pride, Countee Cullen's spirituality, and Langston
Hughes's dedication to music. Brooks's earliest poems show
an awareness of the positive qualities in Black life. She
changed, however, from an initial emphasis on the private
experience of Negroes to her present concern with communal
relationships and militant expression. Brooks adheres to
the essentially American ideals of individual dignity and
freedom for all.

5   JOHNSON, JAMES WELDON. "August 30, 1937," in <u>Report from Part
One</u>. Edited by Gwendolyn Brooks. Detroit: Broadside
Press, p. 201.
[To Brooks] Continue your writing of verse, and read
the best modern poets simultaneously. These actions will
help you to cultivate the highest standards of self-criticism.

6   KENT, GEORGE E. "Gwen's Way," in <u>Report from Part One</u>.
Edited by Gwendolyn Brooks. Detroit: Broadside Press,
pp. 32-33.
Brooks strikes a good balance between the mode of con-
fession and that of memoir. Her lyricism comes from human-
ism, her "acknowledgment of the irreducible measure of
aloneness borne by man and woman alike." Upon chaos Brooks
imposes the creative image.

7   LEE, DON L. "The Achievement of Gwendolyn Brooks," <u>Black
Scholar</u>, 3 (Summer), 32-41.
Gwendolyn Brooks's poetry after 1967 is lean. In view-
ing the earlier work, you see a poet on the road to African
consciousness or blackness. With the possible exception
of Margaret Walker, her work has a stronger sense of self-
awareness than does the literature of her contemporaries.
Like the verses of Langston Hughes, hers have concerned
the problems of Black America. In the late fifties and
early sixties, her verse appealed to a wide audience, and
her reach was like that of James Baldwin or Ralph Ellison.
Before the women liberationists of the 1970's, Brooks gave
Black women their due. In <u>Mecca</u>, she experimented with

blank or free verse, and the title poem was to be her "epic of black humanity." With the publication of <u>Riot</u>, Brooks began her association with Broadside Press, one of the "newest and most significant black publishing companies in the world." Her association with the young influenced her present work, as did a trip to East Africa in 1971. Revised 1972.B8.

8   <u>   </u>. "Gwendolyn Brooks: Beyond the Wordmaker--The Making of an African Poet," in <u>Report from Part One</u>. Edited by Gwendolyn Brooks. Detroit: Broadside Press, pp. 13-30.
    In the early years, iambic pentameter strains Brooks's poetic song. She is "conditioned." <u>Annie Allen</u>, more than <u>A Street in Bronzeville</u>, was written for whites. Although some may find the title poem of <u>Annie Allen</u> to be earth-shaking, it "leaves me completely dry." With <u>Mecca</u> comes a loss of verbal excess and more experimentation in free or blank verse. <u>Mecca</u>, her "epic of black humanity," includes all the indications of her craft: prose verse, off-rhyme, random rhyme, couplet, and ballad. With <u>Riot</u> (1969), Brooks began her association with Broadside Press. Slight revision of 1972.B7

9   McKAY, CLAUDE. "October 10, 1945," in <u>Report from Part One</u>. Edited by Gwendolyn Brooks. Detroit: Broadside Press.
    Congratulations on the publication of <u>A Street in Bronzeville</u> and welcome to the rank of hard-working poets who have something to say. Although we must travel a difficult road, one derives compensation from the ability to sing.

10   RANDALL, DUDLEY. "The Black Aesthetic in the Thirties, Forties and Fifties," in <u>The Black Aesthetic</u>. Edited by Addison Gayle, Jr. New York: Anchor Books, pp. 212-221.
    Brooks, like Hayden and Tolson, is a poet who is con- scious of craft and who has learned from the modern masters of experimentation--Crane, Eliot, Pound, and Yeats. In <u>A Street in Bronzeville</u> Brooks wrote about black people on the South Side of Chicago, but also about men at war, espe- cially in the sonnets. <u>Annie Allen</u> shows a mastery of the ballad, and of the fourteen-line form, which she makes crisp. Like Tolson and Hayden she firmly controls the long poem. Now at the height of their powers, Hayden and Brooks can still change and grow.

11   REHM, BARBARA. "Pulitzer Prize Poetess, 'Old, Inarticulate at 55,'" <u>PP</u> (August 27), p. E1.

Brooks writes because she is inarticulate orally. From blues and funeral chants, her verse reaches to the high laughter of the city.

12   TANCILL, KAREN. "Poet Laureate of Illinois Gives Reading at Dominican," RJT (December 6), p. 7A.
       Brooks does not want to be put on a pedestal. The poetry that she read Tuesday night was "blunt, straight-forward, and concise."

1973 A BOOKS - NONE

1973 B SHORTER WRITINGS

1   ANON. "Gwendolyn Brooks's Tribute," BlackW (July), p. 86.
       Brooks deserves the title of "Mother of the New Black Poets."

2   BOMBARA, TONI CADE. "Report from Part One," NYTBR, (January), Sec. 7, p. 1.
       Although Brooks's work is now more communal than private, "change" or "shift" may be too strong a word. Rereading her work shows a continuum. Report from Part One is a loose assemblage of photographs, interviews, and letters. In Brooks's fiftieth year one found a development of style: movement and energy, intensity, richness, power of state-ment, and compression. Since the late sixties, Brooks has resembled the younger black poets. She has sought the idiom, cadence, and style that will politicize and mobilize. Her recent work moves toward gesture, sound, and intonation. Such qualities call for oral presentation rather than "private eyeballing." See also 1950.B13.

3   HANSELL, WILLIAM H. "Aestheticism Versus Political Militancy in Gwendolyn Brooks's 'The Chicago Picasso" and 'The Wall,'" CLAJ, 17 (September), 11-15.
       Each poem gives a "radically different view of art." "The Wall" shows that Brooks's purpose is to write about black people and for a black audience. She has adopted a black mystique. The meaning of "Chicago Picasso," how-ever, is that art is self-justifying.

4   HENDERSON, STEVEN, ed. "Introduction," in Understanding the New Black Poetry. New York: William Morrow, p. 26.
       Brooks, like Mari Evans and Robert Hayden, moves outside of the "immediate concerns of the black community." Her quest is for self-revelation. With other Black writers--

1973

    Margaret Walker, Robert Hayden, and Dudley Randall--she
shares a mastery of the ballad. All have added to the
Anglo-American tradition of Dante Rossetti and William
Morris.

5   HUDSON, CLENORA F. "Racial Themes in the Poetry of Gwendolyn
    Brooks," CLAJ, 17 (September), 16-20.
      Selected Poems gives an excellent commentary on Black
suffering in a racist society. The following verses concern the nature of racism: "De Witt Williams on His Way
to Lincoln Cemetery," "We Real Cool," "The Chicago Defender
Sends a Man to Little Rock," and "The Ballad of Rudolph
Reed." A second category concerns the moods and reactions
of Blacks: (a) the frustration of the old, and (b) the
commentary on the fermentation of restless youths. Among
the latter, one finds such verses as "Negro Hero," "The
Progress," and "The Certainty We Two Shall Meet By God."

6   LOFF, JON N. "Gwendolyn Brooks: A Bibliography," CLAJ, 17
    (September), 21-32.
      To date, this is the definitive bibliography on the works
of Gwendolyn Brooks. It lists publications by and about the
author. The first two sections are chronological, but the
remaining five are alphabetical: I. Brooks's volumes of
poetry and prose, with availability and prices; II. Separate publications in periodicals and newspapers (no pages
given for those in the morgue of CDN, CST, or CT); III.
Four personal interviews; IV. Listing of various secondary
books; V. Reviews and articles in journals and newspapers;
VI. Records, tapes, and films of Brooks's literary per-
formances; and VII. Three graduate studies, unpublished.

7   RANDALL, DUDLEY. "To Gwendolyn Brooks, Teacher," BlackW
    (February), p. 53.
      Her life is a lesson to blacks.

8   RILEY, FURMAN. "Gwendolyn Brooks: The Unconditioned Poet,"
    CLAJ, 17 (September), 1-10.
      Brooks's poetry has begun to reflect her championing of
a Black identity that is positive. One should read In the
Mecca (1968), Riot (1969) and Family Pictures (1970) to-
gether, since all indicate the poet's response to changes
in the Black community. Compare 1971.B8.

9   SHANDS, ANNETTE OLIVER. "Gwendolyn Brooks as Novelist,"
    BlackW (June), pp. 22-30.
      In Maud Martha Brooks presents the ideas and techniques
that appear in her poems, but the novel has less subtlety.

Her themes are varied: sexual interactions, interracial
relations, impressions of the Black community, and per-
plexing questions about mankind.

10 _____. "Report from Part One," BlackW (March), pp. 70-71.
This volume affirms the new woman that is Gwendolyn
Brooks.

11 WASHINGTON, MARY HELEN. "Report from Part One: The Autobiography of Gwendolyn Brooks," BlackW (March), pp. 51-52,
70.
For the seventies, this is an important and powerful
document. Brooks helps to build a Black institution
[undefined] as black artists or writers should.

1974 A BOOKS - NONE

1974 B SHORTER WRITINGS

1 BAKER, HOUSTON A., JR. "The Achievement of Gwendolyn Brooks,"
in Singers of Daybreak. Washington, D.C.: Howard University Press, pp. 43-51.
Reprints 1972.B1.

2 DAVIS, ARTHUR P. "Gwendolyn Brooks," in From the Dark Tower.
Washington: Howard University Press, pp. 185-193.
Her work has never been simple, but it has grown more
difficult through the years. Like Tolson, she has changed
her style and viewpoint in mid-career. Of her first three
volumes, much of the work was protest: subtly ironic and
quietly humorous, but never strident, rhetorical, or bitter. Brooks speaks sharply on the theme of color prejudice
within the race, especially as it applies to a dark-skinned
woman. Most pieces concerned with this motif are written
in the ballad form. With the publication of In the Mecca,
Gwendolyn Brooks began a new period in her literary career.
Now under the influence of the Black Aesthetics movement,
she has a commitment to blackness that is very evident in
her last two books. The "pathetic little story" of the
title poem in Mecca is secondary to Brooks's penetration
into the lives and thoughts of her characters. Maud Martha
is one of her "most sensitive and understanding works."
Like Robert Hayden, Brooks is a brilliant craftsman in
verse. Her shift in style parallels her shift in ideol-
ogy. In the later work, she abandons many conventional
forms used earlier (tercets and variants of Chaucer's rime
royal). Like most modern poets, she now employs rhyme

1974

sparingly. Brooks weaves a "brilliant poetic tapestry."
To almost any subject, she brings the freshness and excite-
ment that characterize good poetry.

3   HANSELL, WILLIAM. "Gwendolyn Brooks's In the Mecca: A Re-
      birth into Blackness," NALF, 8 (Summer), 199-217.
         In the Mecca shows Brooks in her third and latest phase.
      Emphasis on blackness [undefined] distinguishes these poems
      from those of the previous period. If her earlier work
      probed private experience, this one discovers communal sig-
      nificance. Throughout the poem, the narrator uses a breadth
      of tones. Mrs. Sallie is a counterpart to Arthur; John Tom,
      to Tennessee; and Hyena, to Alfred. By his imagined rape
      and torture of white Americans, Amos is linked to the
      murderer of Pepitia.

4   _____. "The Role of Violence in Recent Poems of Gwendolyn
      Brooks," SBL, 5 (Summer), 21-27.
         Riot extends In the Mecca; both works attempt to portray
      the "cause and significance of violence." Ideals and
      values are rooted in blackness, or self-identity, and
      love is the central means for social change. From the Book
      of Amos, Brooks may take darkness as a metaphor. In re-
      sponse to the status quo, violence is right, if nothing
      else can convince white America of this nation's tolerance
      for evil.

5   JACKSON, BLYDEN and LOUIS D. RUBIN, JR. Black Poetry in
      America. Baton Rouge: Louisiana State University Press,
      pp. 81-85.
         Brooks speaks constantly of women but sublimates race
      and sex into universal insights and revelations. As a
      master of technique, Brooks has easily assimilated certain
      avant-garde conventions. She writes on no "big subjects"
      [undefined]. Annie Allen typifies her method: the study
      of the flower in the crannied wall; the microcosm of indi-
      vidual experience as a macrocosm of universal life.

6   MADHUBUTI, SAFISHA N. "Focus on Form in Gwendolyn Brooks,"
      Black Books Bulletin, 2, No. 1, 25-27.
         Family Pictures shows techniques basic to Brooks's
      approach--repetition, rhythm, image, and contrast. This
      work is a personal, familial, and cultural statement. It
      is consistent with her earlier life-style and work.

7   MAHONEY, HEIDI L. "Selected Checklist of Material By and About
      Gwendolyn Brooks," NALF, 8 (Summer), 210-211.

126

Primary texts are outlined as follows: I. Major Works (17); II. Manuscript Collections (27); and III. Recordings (5). Secondary works are outlined as follows: I. Criticism (articles, 14); and II. Reviews of individual works (64).

8   TOWNS, SAUNDRA. "Black Autobiography and the Dilemma of Western Artistic Tradition," <u>Black Books Bulletin</u>, 2, No. 1, 17-23.
      Its structure makes <u>Report from Part One</u> unique: memos, notations, interviews, and letters. It leads us into the private and captivating world of Brooks's imagination. Having gained a larger consciousness, Brooks assesses her past in light of her present. The structure of the volume reflects Brooks's attempt to combine the roles of poet and political person.

<u>1975 A BOOKS - NONE</u>

<u>1975 B SHORTER WRITINGS</u>

1   HULL, GLORIA T. "A Note on the Poetic Technique of Gwendolyn Brooks," <u>CLAJ</u>, 19, No. 2 (December), 280-285.
      Critics have long recognized Brooks's stature, but rarely have evaluated her work on the basis of style or technique. Her technical qualities are diction and tone, syntax and sentence structure, economy of words, and minor techniques like alliteration and rhyme. By using these in an individual way, she creates a distinct voice.

2   TOWNS, SAUNDRA. "<u>Beckonings</u>," <u>BlackW</u>, 25, No. 2, 51-52.
      Gwendolyn Brooks faces the challenge of creating history as spirit or myth. In past works such as <u>Maud Martha</u>, with its white values, she failed to examine the "why of things." Although <u>In the Mecca</u> reflected the vitality and optimism of the sixties, the verses in <u>Beckonings</u> indicate the disillusionment and questioning of the seventies. Chaos and strife test a feminine sensibility that needs stability, order, and beauty.

<u>1976 A BOOKS - NONE</u>

<u>1976 B SHORTER WRITINGS</u>

1   HANSELL, WILLIAM H. "Gwendolyn Brooks's Collections: <u>Family Pictures</u> and <u>Beckonings</u>," paper delivered at the 4th Annual

1976

Conference on Minority Studies. La Crosse: University of
Wisconsin, April 30. On cassette.
    Considered thematically, Family Pictures and Beckonings
greatly resemble Brooks's verses published in the late sixties. Her work of the seventies looks back to Riot and
Mecca. Throughout Brooks's career, the black hero has been
a consideration. Reprinted 1977.B1.

2   MILLER, R. BAXTER. "Define the Whirlwind: In the Mecca--
      Urban Setting, Shifting Narrator, and Redemptive Vision,"
      paper delivered at the 4th Annual Conference on Minority
      Studies. La Crosse: University of Wisconsin, April 30.
      On cassette. Obsidian (scheduled, Winter, 1978).
        Mecca is one of the most "complex and intriguing volumes
      of this century." With the sordid reality of urban life,
      it balances an imaginative process of reconciliation and
      redemption. On three points one can evaluate the effec-
      tiveness of the volume: Anglo-American tradition, paradox
      of the American Dream, and skillful uses of technique
      (Christian myth, parody, varying distance of narration).
      Brooks's greatest talent may be the creation of different
      viewpoints within one poetic world. From deep within
      Black American experience, she expresses the universality
      outside.

1977 A BOOKS - NONE

1977 B SHORTER WRITINGS

1   HANSELL, WILLIAM H. "Essences, Unifyings, and Black Militancy:
      Major Themes in Gwendolyn Brooks's Family Pictures and
      Beckonings," BALF, 11 (Summer) 63-66.
        Reprints 1976.B1.

Index

Index to Langston Hughes

131

Cargill, Oscar, 1941.B2
Carmen, Y., 1939.B1
Carmon, Walt, 1930.B1
"The Cat and the Saxophone"
    (poem), 1971.B5
Chandler, G. Lewis, 1949.B1;
    1951.B1
Chicago Defender (newspaper),
    1971.A1, B3; 1973.B2
"Christ in Alabama" (poem),
    1967.B21; 1968.B8; 1973.B2
"Christ in Alabama: Religion in
    the Poetry of Langston
    Hughes," 1973.B2
Clarke, John Henrik, 1963.B3
Cobb, Martha K., 1975.B1
Collier, Eugene W., 1971.A2, B3
Column, Mary M., 1942.B2
"Comic Elements in Selected Prose
    Works by James Baldwin, Ralph
    Ellison, and Langston
    Hughes," 1972.B1
"Common Clay and Poetry,"
    1927.B6
Concordance to Langston Hughes,
    1975.A1
Cook, Mercer, 1969.B3
Cook, Meyer, 1971.B14
Cooperman, Stanley, 1952.B4
"Cora Unashamed" (short story),
    1934.B3, B6; 1966.B2; 1970.A2
Creekmore, Hubert, 1947.B2
The Crisis (periodical), 1968.B5
"A Critical Analysis," 1968.B6
Cuban, Larry, 1964.B2
Cullen, Countee, 1924.B2; 1926.B2

D

Daiches, David, 1949.B2
"A Danish Tribute to Langston
    Hughes," 1968.B16
Dark Symphony, 1968.B7
Davis, Arthur P., 1941.B1;
    1952.B5; 1954.B3; 1955.B4;
    1966.B1; 1968.B4; 1970.B3;
    1971.B4; 1974.B2
Davis, Charles T., 1970.B4
"Daybreak in Alabama" (poem),
    1967.B21; 1976.B3
"Death in Harlem" (poem),
    1942.B2
"The Death of Simple," 1967.B1

Deutsch, Babette, 1927.B2;
    1951.B2
The Devil, the Gargoyle, and the
    Buffoon, 1969.B6
Diakhaté, Lamine, 1967.B11
Dialect poems, 1926.B3; 1927.B2,
    B8; See also The Blues, Jazz
    poems
"Dialogues but Barbed," 1950.B7
Dickinson, Donald C., 1964.A1;
    1965.B1; 1968.B5; 1972.A1
"Did Van Vechten Make or Take
    Hughes' Blues?" 1976.B1
Dillard, Irving, 1962.B2
Diop, David, 1971.B14
Dodat, François, 1967.B12
Dodson, Owen, 1942.B3
"'Done Made Us Leave Our Home':
    Langston Hughes's Not Without
    Laughter--Unifying Image and
    Three Dimensions," 1976.B2
Don't You Want to be Free (play),
    1938.B1; 1967.B26; 1971.B17
"Dream Deferred: A Comment on
    Langston Hughes's Poetry,"
    1973.B4
The Dream Keeper and Other Poems,
    1932.B1, B3
Drew, Fraser, 1959.B4
Du Bois, W. E. B., 1924.B1

E

Eaton, Anne T., 1932.B3
"Elderly Leaders" (poem), 1971.B5
Emanuel, James A., 1961.B2;
    1966.B2; 1967.A1, B13;
    1968.B6-B9; 1971.A2, B5-B6;
    1973.B2
Embree, Edwin R., 1941.B3;
    1944.B1
Emperor of Haiti (play), 1971.B17
Evans, Mari, 1967.B14
"'Even After I was Dead': The
    Big Sea - Paradox, Preserva-
    tion, and Holistic Time,"
    1977.B1

F

The Faithless Wife (translation),
    1971.B14

Guillén, Nicholás, 1967.B19
"Guitar" (short story), 1959.B10

H

H., V., 1955.B6
Hansell, William Harold, 1972.B8
Harlem, 1926.B3-B4; 1942.B2;
    1952.B5; 1959.B8; 1966.B1;
    1968.B4; 1970.B4
"The Harlem of Langston Hughes's
    Poetry," 1952.B5; 1966.B1
Hatch, Robert R., 1955.B7
Hawthorne, Lucia Sheila, 1971.A1
Hays, H. R., 1942.B4
Hedden, Worth Tuttle, 1952.B6
"He Knew the Street," 1967.B8
Henderson, Stephen E., 1969.B3
Hentoff, Nat, 1958.B4
Herod, Henrietta L., 1941.B5
Heyward, Du Bose, 1926.B4;
    1927.B5
Hill, Roy L., 1973.B3
Holmes, Eugene C., 1934.B5;
    1968.B12
"Home" (short story), 1934.B3;
    1961.B2
"How the Money Rolled In,"
    1958.B3
Hudson, Theodore R., 1968.B13
"Hughes at Columbia," 1967.B3
"Hughesesque Insight," 1950.B5
"Hughes on Jazz," 1955.B2
"Humor and Hope," 1958.B2
Humphries, Rolfe, 1949.B3;
    1951.B3

I

"The Image of the White Man in
    the Fiction of Langston
    Hughes, Richard Wright,
    James Baldwin, and Ralph
    Ellison," 1968.B2
"In Memoriam to a Beloved
    Friend," 1967.B26
Intellectual America: Ideas on
    the March, 1941.B2
"Introduction," Five Plays by
    Langston Hughes, 1968.B24

"Introduction," Langston Hughes:
    Un Chant Nouveau, 1940.B2
"Introduction," Seven Poets in
    Search of an Answer, 1944.B2
"I Remember Langston," 1967.B14
Isaacs, Harold, 1960.B2
"Isolation in Langston Hughes,"
    1970.B6
"I Teach Negro Literature,"
    1941.B4
Ivy, James, W., 1956.B1; 1959.B5
I Wonder as I Wander, 1956.B2,
    B4; 1956.B6; 1957.B2, B4

J

Jackson, Blyden, 1959.B6;
    1968.B14; 1970.B5; 1971.A2;
    1974.B3
Jackson, Irma Wertz, 1964.B3
Jackson, Luther, 1957.B4-B5
Jacobs, Leland, 1964.B4
Jahn, Janheinz, 1958.B5; 1961.B5;
    1968.B15
"Jazz as a Marching Jubilee,"
    1961.B1
"The Jazz Band's Sob," 1926.B4
"Jazz Consciousness," 1934.B7
Jazz poems, 1926.B1; 1949.B2;
    1961.B1; 1969.B6, B14;
    1974.B2-B3; See also The
    Blues, Dialect poems
Jemie, Onwuchekwa, 1973.B4;
    1976.A1
"Jesse B. Semple and the Narra-
    tive Art of Langston Hughes,"
    1973.B5
"Jesse B. Semple: Negro American,"
    1954.B3
"Jesse B. Semple Revisited and
    Revised," 1971.B2
"Jim Crow Car" (poem), 1967.B21
Joans, Ted, 1972.B9
Johnson, James Weldon, 1930.B5
Johnson, Lemuel A., 1969.B6
Jones, Eldred, 1967.B20
Jones, Harry L., 1968.B16;
    1971.A2, B10
"Justice Comes High," 1962.B4

"Langston Hughes: Poet of the Negro Renaissance," 1972.B7

"Langston Hughes: Poet of the People," 1939.B1

"Langston Hughes's First Short Story: Mary Winosky," 1961.B2

"Langston Hughes's Jesse B. Semple: A Black Walter Mitty," 1976.B6

"Langston Hughes's Jesse B. Semple and the Blues," 1975.B2

"Langston Hughes's Jesse B. Semple: The Urban Negro as Wise Fool," 1969.B8

"Langston Hughes Speaks to Young Writers," 1946.B1

"Langston Hughes: The First Book of Jazz," 1955.B6

"Langston Hughes: The Minstrel as Artificer," 1975.B5

"Langston Hughes," 13 Against the Odds, 1944.B1

Laughing to Keep from Crying, 1952.B3-B6, B8-B10

"Laughing to Keep from Crying," 1967.B20

"Laughter and Tears Across the Barriers of Race," 1952.B6

"Laughter, Tears, and the Blues," 1952.B9

"Laura and Essie Belle," 1958.B6

Lechlinter, Ruth, 1947.B3

Lee Ulysses, 1963.B2

"Le Souvenir de Langston Hughes," 1967.B19

"Let America Be America Again" (poem), 1962.B3; 1963.B7

Lewis, Theophilus, 1940.B3

The Liberation of American Literature, 1932.B2

"Limiting Devices," 1927.B3

"Lincoln's Man of Letters," 1964.B5

"The Literary Experiments of Langston Hughes," 1968.B8; 1971.A2, B5

"The Literary Landscape," 1934.B2

"Literature of the Negro Ghetto," 1952.B10

"A Little Colored Boy Grows Up," 1930.B7

"Little Dog" (short story), 1966.B2

Little Ham (play), 1971.B17

Littlejohn, David, 1966.B3

Lloyd, Hortense D., 1952.B7

Locke, Alain, 1925.B1; 1926.B5; 1927.B6-B7; 1934.B6

Loggins, Vernon, 1934.B7

Long, Richard A., 1959.B7; 1963.B3-B4

Lowery, Delitta Martin, 1975.B3

Lucas, Bob, 1967.B23

M

McBrown, Gertrude P., 1953.B5

McGhee, Nancy B., 1971.A2, B12

MacLeod, Norman, 1938.B1

McPherson, James M., 1971.B13

"The Major Theme in Langston Hughes's Not Without Laughter," 1970.B7

Mandelik, Peter, 1975.A1

"The Man Who Created Simple," 1967.B22

Margolies, Edward, 1968.B19

"Mary Winosky" (short story), 1961.B2

Masters of the Dew, 1951.B2-B5; 1970.B4; 1973.B8

Matheus, John F., 1968.B20; 1971.A2, B14

Mayfield, Julian, 1967.B24

Meier, August, 1952.B8

Meltzer, Milton, 1968.A1; 1969.B7

Mercy of Circumstances (play), 1964.B7

"'A Mere Poem': 'Daybreak in Alabama,' a Resolution to Langston Hughes's Theme of Music and Art," 1976.B3

Merlin, Robert T., 1924.B2

"Mexican Market Woman" (poem), 1964.B4

Miles, William, 1970.B6

The Militant Black Writers, 1969.B3

Miller, Johnine B., 1970.B7

Miller, R. Baxter, 1975.B4; 1976.B2-B5; 1977.B1

O'Daniel, Therman B., 1951.B4;
    1964.B5; 1968.B22; 1971.A2,
    B15–B16
"Odyssey of a Literary Man,"
    1957.B2
"Of Myth and Symbol," 1947.B4
"Old Clothes," 1927.B11
"One Friday Morning" (short
    story), 1952.B7
"One-Way Poetry," 1949.B5
One Way Ticket, 1948.B3; 1949.B1–
    B3, B5; 1951.B1
"On the Road" (short story),
    1966.B2
"On the Way Home" (short story),
    1961.B2
"Open Handshake," 1954.B3
O'Sheel, Thomas Yoseloff, 1944.B2
"Other Opinions of the Nineteen
    Thirties," Soviet Attitudes
    Toward American Writing,
    1962.B1
Ottley, Roi, 1956.B2
"Our Book Shelf," 1926.B3
Ovington, Mary White, 1927.B9

P

"A Pain in this Soul: Simple as
    Epic Hero," 1971.A2, B3
"A Pair of Youthful Negro Poets,"
    1924.B2
The Pamphlet Poets, 1927.B7
The Panther and the Lash: Poems
    of Our Times, 1967.B21–B22;
    1968.B4, B8, B10, B13
"Parcels of Humanity," 1956.B4
Parker, John W., 1949.B4;
    1951.B5; 1952.B10; 1955.B9;
    1956.B3–B4; 1957.B7–B9;
    1959.B8–B9; 1961.B6
Patterson, Lindsay, 1968.B23
"Paying for Old Sins," 1934.B1
Peterkin, Julia, 1927.B10
Pfaff, William, 1950.B2
Pictorial History of the Negro in
    America, 1956.B1, B5; 1957.B1
Piquion, René, 1940.A1
Plays, 1963.B8; 1964.B7;
    1967.B24; 1968.B23–B24;
    1971.A2, B17; See also indi-
    vidual plays and collections

"Poemas," 1952.B1
"Poems by Langston Hughes,"
    1947.B2
Poems from Black Africa,
    1963.B4–B5; 1971.B14
"Poems to Play: Langston Hughes
    Describes the Genius of His
    Tambourines to Glory,"
    1963.B6
"A Poet Asks: How Long is a
    While?" 1962.B2
"The Poetic Faith of a Social
    Poet," 1959.B9
"Poet on Poet," 1926.B2
"The Poet Who Invented Soul,"
    1967.B23
Poetry, 1924.B1–B2; 1925.B1;
    1926.B1; 1927.B7, B9, B11;
    1929.B1; 1930.B6; 1932.B1–B2;
    1933.B1; 1938.B1; 1940.A1, B1,
    B3; 1941.B4; 1944.B2; 1947.B3;
    1949.B5; 1958.B4, B5; 1959.B1,
    B3, B9, B12; 1960.B2; 1963.B7;
    1964.B3; 1968.B4, B18;
    1969.B7; 1970.B4; 1971.A2, B1,
    B9–B10; 1972.B5, B7–B8;
    1973.B5; 1974.B1–B3; 1975.B1;
    1976.B1, B3–B4; See also The
    Blues, Dialect poems, Jazz
    poems and individual poems
    and collections
"The Poetry and Argument of
    Langston Hughes," 1938.B1
"Poetry of Harlem in Transition,"
    1951.B5
"Poetry of Negro Moods," 1949.B2
The Poetry of the Negro, 1746–
    1949, 1971.B14
"A Poet's Debut as Novelist,"
    1930.B2
"A Poet's Story," 1941.B3
"Poignancy," 1952.B8
"Politics, Poetry, and Peccadil-
    los," 1956.B2
Poore, Charles, 1965.B4
Porgy and Bess, 1969.B11
"The Portrait of the Artist as a
    Black American in the Poetry
    of Langston Hughes," 1974.B1
Portraits in Color, 1927.B9
"Positive Themes in the Poetry of
    Four Negroes," 1972.B8

Potamkin, Harry Alan, 1927.B11
"Powder White Faces" (short
    story), 1968.B9
Presley, James, 1963.B7;
    1969.B11; 1973.B6
Prodigal Son (play), 1967.B25
"The Professor" (short story),
    1941.B1; 1952.B7; 1973.B1
"Profile: Langston Hughes,"
    1964.B3
"Proposition" (poem), 1964.B4
Prowle, Allen D., 1969.B12

Q

Quinot, Raymond, 1964.A2

R

Rabearivelo, Jean Joseph,
    1971.B14
Randall, Dudley, 1967.B27;
    1972.B10
"Real and Artificial Folk Song,"
    1927.B8
Redding, J. Saunders, 1930.B6;
    1950.B3; 1951.B6; 1956.B5-B6
"Red Headed Baby" (short story),
    1961.B2
"The Remarkable Mr. Simple
    Again," 1957.B7
"Reviewing Stand," 1969.B13
"Rhetorical Embellishment in
    Hughes's Simple Stories,"
    1971.A2, B10
A Rhetoric of Human Rights as
    Expressed in the 'Simple
    Columns,' by Langston Hughes,
    1971.A1
Rivers, Clarence J., 1964.B7
"Robert Burns and Langston
    Hughes," 1968.B18
Rollins, Charlemae Hill,
    1965.B5; 1970.A2
Rosenblatt, Roger, 1974.B4
Ross, Mary, 1930.B7
"Round About Parnassus," 1932.B1
Rubin, Louis D., Jr., 1974.B3
Rugoff, Milton, 1940.B4

S

"Satire in the Work of Langston
    Hughes," 1972.B3
Scarnhorst, Gary F., 1973.B7
Schatt, Stanley, 1975.A1, B5
Schoell, F. L., 1929.B1
Schleifer, Marc, 1964.B6
"Search for Identity: A Critical
    Survey of Significant Belles
    Lettres By and About Negroes
    Published in 1961," 1962.B3
"Selected Bibliography of the
    Published Writings of
    Langston Hughes," 1968.B17
"A Selected List of Children's
    Books," 1969.B5
Selected Poems (Mistral),
    1971.B14
Selected Poems of Langston
    Hughes, 1959.B3, B9, B12
"Selected Poems of Nicolás
    Guillén and Langston Hughes,"
    1975.B3
"Selfsameness and a Promise,"
    1949.B1
"Sepia Deb Ball," 1964.B6
Sergeant, Elizabeth, 1926.B6
"Sermons and Blues," 1959.B1
"Seven American Poets," 1942.B5
Shagaloff, June, 1953.B6
Shakespeare in Harlem, 1942.B1-
    B6; 1951.B1; 1959.B3
"Shakespeare in Harlem," 1942.B3
"The Short Fiction of Langston
    Hughes," 1968.B9; 1971.A2, B6
Short stories, 1941.B1; 1948.B2;
    1962.B2; 1966.B2; 1967.B14,
    B27; 1968.B2, B6-B7, B9;
    1971.A2; 1973.B4; See also
    individual stories and
    collections
"The Short Stories of Langston
    Hughes," 1966.B2; 1967.A1
"The Significant Influence of
    Langston Hughes on the Think-
    ing and the Inner Lives of
    Nine Contemporary Black
    Poets," 1973.B3
Simple Columns, 1971.A1
"Simple's Dialogues," 1950.B4

Index to Gwendolyn Brooks

Bird, Leonard G., 1969.B3
Bishop, Claire Huchet, 1956.B5
"The Black Aesthetic in the
    Thirties, Forties and
    Fifties," 1972.B10
"The Black and Tan Motif in the
    Poetry of Gwendolyn Brooks,"
    1962.B5
"Black Autobiography and the
    Dilemma of Western Artistic
    Tradition," 1974.B8
"Black Poetry," 1969.B9
Black Poetry in America, 1974.B5
"Black Pulitzer Awareness,"
    1970.B8
Blacks in America, 1971.B10
Bock, Frederick, 1960.B5
Bombara, Toni Cade, 1973.B2
Bontemps, Arna, 1969.B4
"Books for Young Adults,"
    1971.B2
"Books That Look Out, Books That
    Look In," 1969.B11
Bradley, Van Allen, 1949.B6;
    1953.B5; 1956.B6; 1962.B3;
    1963.B12-B13
"Bronze by Gold," 1950.B21
"Bronzeville," 1945.B6
Bronzeville Boys and Girls,
    1956.B1-B5, B8-B9; 1957.B1,
    B3
"A Bronzeville Mother Loiters in
    Mississippi, Meanwhile a
    Mississippi Mother Burns
    Bacon" (poem), 1960.B1, B7-
    B8; 1961.B3; 1962.B8; 1971.B9
"Brooks, Gwendolyn," 1971.B3
Brown, Frank London, 1961.B2
Brown, Patricia L., 1971.B12
Bureke, Christian E., 1950.B17
Burke, Herbert, 1960.B6
Burroughs, Margaret T., 1971.B5
Butcher, Fanny, 1953.B6

C

"Cellini-like Lyrics," 1949.B10
"The Certainty We Two Shall Meet
    By God" (poem), 1973.B5
Cherry, Gwendolyn, 1962.B4
"Chicago," 1952.B1

"Chicago a Harbor for Anyone Who
    Comes Here," 1962.B8
"The Chicago Defender Sends a Man
    to Little Rock" (poem),
    1963.B14; 1973.B5
"The Chicago Picasso" (poem),
    1969.B2; 1973.B3
"'Chicago Poem' Jury at Work,"
    1963.B12
"Chicago Poet Wins $1,000 Arts
    Prize," 1946.B1
"Chicago's Finest Writers,"
    1949.B8
"Chicago's Great Lady of Poetry,"
    1961.B2
"Children of the Poor" (poem),
    1971.B9
"Chi Poet Wins Pulitzer Prize,"
    1950.B2
"City Has Fifth of Nation's Most
    Influential Negroes," 1963.B2
Clyde, Glenda E., 1966.A1
"Cold Doesn't Deter Poets from
    Rounds," 1958.B3
Contemporary Authors, 1962.B6
Crockett, Jacqueline, 1955.B1
Cromie, Robert, 1964.B21
Cullen, Countee, 1972.B2
Cutler, Bruce, 1963.B14

D

Dana, Robert Patrick, 1961.B3
Dark Symphony, 1968.B3
Davis, Arthur P., 1962.B5;
    1969.B5; 1974.B2
Davis, Charles T., 1970.B1
"Define...the Whirlwind: In the
    Mecca--Urban Setting, Shift-
    ing Narrator, and Redemptive
    Vision," 1976.B2
"Depres to Talk Here at College
    Commencement," 1964.B1
Derleth, August, 1957.B3
Deutsch, Babette, 1950.B15
"De Witt Williams on His Way to
    Lincoln Cemetery" (poem),
    1973.B5
"Distinguished Panel to Select
    Top Youths," 1959.B2

"Poetry for Prose Readers,"
1950.B22
"The Poetry of Gwendolyn Brooks,"
1962.B8; 1964.B28
"The Poetry of Gwendolyn Brooks,
Part I," 1971.B8
"The Poetry of Gwendolyn Brooks,
Part II," 1971.B9
"Poetry Prize Winner Got an
Early Start," 1956.B6
"Poetry Winners Named," 1964.B14
"Poet Tells of Life in Bronze-
ville," 1960.B1
"Poet to Talk," 1962.B2
"The Politics of Poetry,"
1969.B8
Portraits in Color, 1962.B4
"Positive Themes in the Poetry
of Four Negroes," 1972.B4
Powers, Irene, 1958.B3
"Prizes," 1944.B1
"A Prize-Winning Poet Fails to
Measure Up," 1960.B5
"Prize-Winning Poet Will Get
College Honor," 1964.B15
"Proclaim Saturday as Poetry
Day," 1963.B6
"The Progress" (poem), 1973.B5
"Public's Impact on Public
Stressed," 1964.B13
"The Pulitzer," 1950.B7
"Pulitzer Poetess at Library
Nov. 2," 1950.B8
"Pulitzer Poet to Lecture at
Northwestern University on
Mid-Century American Poets,"
1964.B16
"Pulitzer Prize Announced by
Columbia University," 1950.B9
"Pulitzer Prize Poetess, 'Old,
Inarticulate at 55,'"
1972.B11
"Pulitzer Prize Winner Joins
Lecture Staff," 1965.B1

Q

"A Quartet of Younger Singers,"
1960.B10

R

"Racial Themes in the Poetry of
Gwendolyn Brooks," 1973.B5
Randall, Dudley, 1969.B9; 1970.B5;
1972.B10; 1973.B7
Ray, David, 1970.B6
The Reader's Encyclopedia of
American Literature, 1955.B2
Redding, J. Saunders, 1949.B10
Rehm, Barbara, 1972.B11
Report from Part One, 1972.B5-B6,
B8-B9; 1973.B2, B10-B11;
1974.B8
"Report from Part One," 1973.B2,
B10
Rexroth, Kenneth, 1964.B27
"Riders to the Blood Red Wrath"
(poem), 1964.B23
Riley, Furman, 1973.B8
Riot, 1970.B2; 1971.B9; 1972.B7;
1973.B8; 1974.B3; 1976.B1
Rivers, Conrad Kent, 1964.B28
Robinson, Donald, 1970.B7
Roethe, Anne, 1950.B23
"The Role of Violence in Recent
Poems of Gwendolyn Brooks,"
1974.B4
Rollins, Charlemae, 1956.B9
Rosenberger, Coleman, 1953.B10
Rosenthal, M. L., 1969.B10
Rubin, Louis D., Jr., 1974.B5

S

Saver, C. M., 1945.B7
"Selected Checklist of Material
By and About Gwendolyn
Brooks," 1974.B7
"A Selected List of Children's
Books," 1956.B5
Selected Poems, 1963.B7-B8, B12,
B14-B15, B19-B21; 1964.B4,
B17, B24, B29
Shands, Annette Oliver, 1973.B9-
B10
Shapiro, Harvey, 1960.B10
Shaw, Harry Bernard, 1972.A2
"She'll Speak to Generations Yet
to Come," 1971.B5

"The Sight of the Horizons"
(poem), 1963.B2
Simpson, Louis, 1963.B21
"Six Poets," 1950.B15
Skeeter, Sharyn J., 1971.B11
"Sketches from Life," 1945.B7
Smith, John Justin, 1962.B7
"Social Comment in Poetry,"
1946.B5
Social Themes in the Poetry of
Gwendolyn Brooks, 1972.A2
"Society of Midland Authors Makes
1963 Book Awards," 1963.B17
"Songs and Funeral Chants,"
1945.B5
"South Pacific Wins 1950 Pulitzer
Prize," 1950.B23
South, Wesley W., 1970.B2
"S-Side Center to Honor Author,"
1946.B2
"S. Siders Honor Pulitzer Poet,"
1950.B11
"S. Side Wife Wins Pulitzer
Poetry Award," 1950.B12
Spector, Robert S., 1964.B29
Stafford, Williams, 1969.B11
A Street in Bronzeville, 1945.B1-
B6, B8; 1946.B3-B5; 1949.B2,
B6-B7, B10; 1950.B18; B20;
1955.B1; 1958.B3; 1960.B4,
B10; 1961.B3; 1962.B8;
1964.B19; 1969.B5; 1971.B8;
1972.B2, B8-B10
"Style and Exasperation,"
1963.B15
"The Sun Salutes Gwendolyn
Brooks," 1946.B3
"The Sundays of Satin-Legs Smith"
(poem), 1945.B5, B7
"Swift, Sharp Prose by a Poet,"
1953.B6

T

Tancill, Karen, 1972.B12
"Tell It Like It Is," 1964.B18
Thomas, Ruby, 1962.B4
"Time of Heterogeneity," 1965.B2
To Be a Black Woman in the Poetry
of Gwendolyn Brooks, 1972.A1
"To Gwendolyn Brooks, Teacher,"
1973.B7
To Gwen With Love, 1971.B1

Toppin, Edgar A., 1969.B12
"Towards a Black Aesthetic,"
1968.B4
Towns, Saundra, 1974.B8; 1975.B2
"12 Arts Advisors Named by
Kerner," 1963.B1
Twentieth Century Authors,
1955.B3
"2 Chicagoans Charm," 1953.B7
"2 Chicago Poets to Appear
February 12 in Loyola Series,"
1958.B1

U

Up From the Ghetto, 1970.B2

V

"A Varied Quartette," 1957.B3
"Verse Chronicle," 1949.B7

W

Walden, Daniel, 1970.B1
"The Wall" (poem), 1973.B3
Ward, Francis, 1971.B12
Warren, Marr, II, 1970.B8
Washington, Mary Helen, 1973.B11
Webster, Harvey Curtis, 1962.B8
"We Real Cool" (poem), 1960.B8;
1971.B6; 1973.B5
Who's Who in Chicago and Illinois,
1950.B13
Who's Who in Colored America,
1950.B17
Who's Who in the Midwest, 1950.B14
Wilder, Amos R., 1945.B7
Willis, Pauline, 1962.B4
"The Womanhood" (poem), 1950.B20;
1966.B2; 1969.B7
"Woman Poet Probes Life of City's
Negroes," 1955.B4
"'Woman of the Year' List Names
Two Chicagoans," 1945.B4
"A Work of Art and Jeweled Pre-
cision," 1953.B10
The World of Gwendolyn Brooks,
1971.B2; 1972.B3

Y

"Yale Conference Studies Role of
Black Women," 1970.B3
"Young Girl Growing Up,"
1953.B9